W9-BKK-862

Thelma Brave

AN INVISIBLE THREAD

AN INVISIBLE THREAD

The True Story of an 11-Year-Old Panhandler, a Busy Sales
Executive, and an Unlikely Meeting with Destiny

LAURA SCHROFF

and *Alex Tresniowski*

HOWARD BOOKS
A DIVISION OF SIMON & SCHUSTER, INC.
New York · Nashville · London · Toronto · Sydney · New Delhi

Howard Books
A Division of Simon & Schuster, Inc.
1230 Avenue of the Americas
New York, NY 10020

Copyright © 2011 by Laura Schroff and Alex Tresniowski

All rights reserved, including the right to reproduce this book or portions thereof in any form whatsoever. For information address Howard Books Subsidiary Rights Department, 1230 Avenue of the Americas, New York, NY 10020.

First Howard Books hardcover edition November 2011

HOWARD and colophon are trademarks of Simon & Schuster, Inc.

For information about special discounts for bulk purchases, please contact Simon & Schuster Special Sales at 1-866-506-1949 or business@simonandschuster.com.

The Simon & Schuster Speakers Bureau can bring authors to your live event. For more information or to book an event, contact the Simon & Schuster Speakers Bureau at 1-866-248-3049 or visit our website at www.simonspeakers.com.

Designed by Ruth Lee-Mui
Edited by Jessica Wong

Manufactured in the United States of America

7   9   10   8

Library of Congress Cataloging-in-Publication Data
Schroff, Laura.
An invisible thread / by Laura Schroff and Alex Tresniowski.
    p.   cm.
1. Schroff, Laura.   2. Mazyck, Maurice.   3. New York (N.Y.)—Biography.
4. Children and adults—Case studies.   5. Friendship—Case studies.   6. African American boys—New York (State)—New York—Biography.   7. Poor children—New York (State)—New York—Biography.   8. Women, White—New York (State)—New York—Biography.
9. Sales executives—New York (State)—New York—Biography.   10. Schroff, Laura—Childhood and youth.   I. Tresniowski, Alex.   II. Title.
F128.56.S37 2011
974.7'1—dc22   2011009636

ISBN 978-1-4516-4251-3
ISBN 978-1-4516-4292-6 (ebook)

All Scripture quotations are from the King James Version of the Bible, public domain.

To all the children like Maurice whose lives are harder than we can imagine. Never lose hope that you can break the cycle and change your life. And never stop dreaming, because the power of dreams can lift you.

CONTENTS

CONTENTS

"An invisible thread connects those who are destined to meet, regardless of time, place, and circumstance. The thread may stretch or tangle. But it will never break."

—Ancient Chinese Proverb

When Laura Schroff walked into my Manhattan office for a job interview in 1978, I was impressed by her confidence and charmed by her personality but, frankly, not overwhelmed. At least not enough to hire her on the spot. I liked her a lot and had a good feeling about her, but I needed to know more—not just about her skills but also about her values. I needed to find out what kind of person she was.

Back then I was associate publisher of *Ms.*, a groundbreaking monthly magazine that debuted in 1972. The idea behind *Ms.* was simple yet profound: we strived to be a catalyst for change in our society. *Ms.* championed gender equality and gave women the courage and inspiration to reach their full potential, make their own choices, and compete in the male-dominated arena of corporate America. Back in the '70s, we weren't living in a world where nearly 40 percent of Harvard Business School graduates are women, as they are today. Nor was Oprah Winfrey on TV five times a week encouraging women to live bolder, fuller lives. Oprah's own inspirational magazine, *O*, wasn't even the germ of an idea in 1978.

In many ways *Ms.* was out there on its own, paving the way for women like Oprah and seeking to empower a generation of future leaders. And this mandate gave those of us who worked at *Ms.* an overwhelming sense of responsibility. We felt we weren't just doing a job—we were helping change the world! As associate publisher, one of my jobs was to hire women to sell advertising pages in the magazine, an essential and challenging job at any magazine but much more so at *Ms.* The flipside to being new and different is having people not quite understand what you stand for, and for a long time the national ad community looked at *Ms.* like a skunk at a picnic. So our salespeople had to work hard to sell not only ad pages but also the message, values, and point of view of the magazine. I needed women who understood this challenge, who shared my devotion to the magazine's vision, who could march into hostile surroundings and change the way people thought. I needed someone with deeply felt values and the courage to fight for them.

And so, when I met Laura, I asked myself this question—does she really care about what we're doing here, or does she just want a job?

I arranged for Laura to come back for a second interview, and that's when I asked her to tell me what mattered to her in life. She didn't hesitate. She talked about her family and her friends, about loyalty and community, about making a difference in people's lives. It became clear to me that Laura was a woman who *cared*. And, as her enthusiasm for what we were doing at *Ms.* clearly showed, she understood the importance of empowering people to dream bigger dreams and lead better lives. Not long after that second interview we offered Laura the job. Not surprisingly, she swept through the ad community with passion and conviction and helped generate tremendous ad growth for the magazine.

And yet, it wasn't until years later that I truly learned how remarkable Laura is.

It was after I left *Ms.* magazine and went to work at *USA Today*, another revolutionary start-up that had to battle for every advertising dollar. As a sales executive there, I had to persuade national brands to take a leap of faith by advertising their products and services in a colorful, broadsheet daily national newspaper, something the country just wasn't used to. The task was daunting, and I realized I needed to hire smart people I trusted. Laura was first on my list. She jumped on board and once again did a phenomenal job, selling millions of dollars worth of advertising in *USA Today*.

But that's not what made me realize how remarkable she is.

Over the years Laura and I became more than business colleagues; we became friends. We ate meals together, discussed boyfriends, went shopping, and did everything friends do. We developed a genuine interest in each other's lives. So it was not surprising that, the Tuesday after Labor Day in 1986, Laura came into my office and told me about something that had happened to her the day before.

I had no way of knowing that the story she told me would one day find its way into this book. I could not have known that the incident she relayed to me would, in my mind, come to define Laura and the kind of person she is. At the time it was just a story, one of many we shared. I doubt either of us believed it would be something we'd still be talking about today, twenty-five years later.

What Laura told me was that, while she was out walking not far from her midtown Manhattan apartment, a little boy, eleven years old, stopped her in the street and asked for spare change. She said the boy had such sad eyes and told her he was really hungry. She said that at first she just walked away, but then, for some reason, she came back. And instead of just giving the boy a quarter, she took him to lunch.

My first reaction was surprise. Personally, I had become so immune to seeing panhandlers on the streets of Manhattan I was reasonably sure I would have kept on walking past the boy and not come back. I admired Laura for what she did. That night we went to dinner together and talked more about this boy—Maurice. I don't think I had ever seen her so animated and excited about anything. Though she had just met this child, she was obviously already invested in his well-being. Something about him, it seemed, had touched her heart.

Over the days and weeks and months that followed we had many more conversations about Maurice, and the more she told me about him the more I realized why Laura was doing what she was doing. But still, to be honest, I wasn't always sure that Laura's involvement with this boy and his horribly dysfunctional family was the right decision for her. I worried that she might come to harm or that what she was doing might be misconstrued. At times I was really angry with her, because I felt she was putting herself at great risk. I wondered if Laura had thought about the huge responsibility she was undertaking. What if her acts of kindness toward Maurice made him dependent on her? What if this unloved and emotionally abused child needed more from her than she could provide? I shared all of these concerns—all of these "what ifs?"—with Laura, often quite forcefully. I felt I had to be a voice of reason for her.

But pretty soon it became clear that Laura wasn't guided by reason. She was guided by faith, conviction, and love.

Laura persuaded me, more through her actions than her words, that she would never abandon Maurice. Over time, in our many talks about him, I realized that Laura—by involving Maurice in some of the simple rituals of her life—was teaching him valuable lessons that would last his lifetime. She told me that no matter what happened to her—no matter how successful she became as an ad sales executive, how busy she was, or how much her own personal life changed—she was committed to Maurice for life. I knew Laura well enough to know these weren't just words. Her commitment to Maurice was not something she took lightly and not something she would ever walk away from.

It was then I finally began to understand just how remarkable Laura's story is.

We live in a cynical world, and sometimes our cynicism gets in the way of seeing things for what they are. My own hard-earned New Yorker's cynicism had prevented me from understanding the special bond between Laura and Maurice, but somehow Laura had seen past all the problems and risks and *unreasonableness* of what she was doing to see it for what it really was—a sweet, heartfelt connection between two people who needed each other.

And now, I couldn't be happier that Laura is sharing her story with the world. I believe there's a powerful message in her small and simple gestures, and I hope you will be as inspired by her story as I have been.

Years ago I remember reading a quote from Dr. Martin Luther King, Jr. He said, "Take the first step in faith. You don't have to see the whole staircase, just take the first step."

Thank you, Laura, for taking that first step with Maurice.

—Valerie Salembier
senior vice president, publisher,
and chief revenue officer
Town&Country

The boy stands alone on a sidewalk in Brooklyn and this is what he sees: a woman running for her life, and another woman chasing her with a hammer. He recognizes one woman as his father's girlfriend. The other, the one with the hammer, he doesn't know.

The boy is stuck in something like hell. He is six years old and covered in small red bites from *chinches*—bedbugs—and he is woefully skinny and malnourished. He is so hungry his stomach hurts, but then being hungry is nothing new to him. When he was two years old the pangs got so bad he rooted through the trash and ate rat droppings and had to have his stomach pumped. He is staying in his father's cramped, filthy apartment in a desolate stretch of Brooklyn, sleeping with stepbrothers who wet the bed, surviving in a place that smells like death. He has not seen his mother in three months, and he doesn't know why. His world is a world of drugs and violence and unrelenting chaos, and he has the wisdom to know, even at six, that if something does not change for him soon, he might not make it.

He does not pray, does not know how, but he thinks, *Please don't let my father let me die.* And this thought, in a way, is its own little prayer.

And then the boy sees his father come up the block, and the woman with the hammer sees him too, and she screams, "Junebug, where is my son?!"

The boy recognizes this voice, and he says, "Mom?"

The woman with the hammer looks down at the boy, and she looks puzzled, until she looks harder and finally says, "Maurice?"

The boy didn't recognize his mother because her teeth had fallen out from smoking dope.

The mother didn't recognize her son because he was so skinny and shriveled.

Now she is chasing Junebug and yelling, "Look what you did to my baby!"

The boy should be frightened, or confused, but more than anything what the boy feels is happiness. He is happy that his mother has come back to get him, and because of that he is not going to die—at least not now, at least not in this place.

He will remember this as the moment when he knew his mother loved him.

AN INVISIBLE THREAD

1

SPARE CHANGE

"Excuse me, lady, do you have any spare change?"

This was the first thing he said to me, on 56th Street in New York City, right around the corner from Broadway, on a sunny September day.

And when I heard him, I didn't really hear him. His words were part of the clatter, like a car horn or someone yelling for a cab. They were, you could say, just noise—the kind of nuisance New Yorkers learn to tune out. So I walked right by him, as if he wasn't there.

But then, just a few yards past him, I stopped.

And then—and I'm still not sure why I did this—I came back.

I came back and I looked at him, and I realized he was just a boy. Earlier, out of the corner of my eye, I had noticed he was young. But now, looking at him, I saw that he was a child—tiny body, sticks for arms, big round eyes. He wore a burgundy sweat-shirt that was smudged and frayed and ratty burgundy sweatpants to match. He had scuffed white sneakers with untied laces, and his fingernails were dirty. But his eyes were bright and there was a general sweetness about him. He was, I would soon learn, eleven years old.

He stretched his palm toward me, and he asked again, "Excuse me, lady, do you have any spare change? I am hungry."

What I said in response may have surprised him, but it really shocked me.

"If you're hungry," I said, "I'll take you to McDonald's and buy you lunch."

"Can I have a cheeseburger?" he asked.

"Yes," I said.

"How about a Big Mac?"

"That's okay, too."

"How about a Diet Coke?"

"Yes, that's okay."

"Well, how about a thick chocolate shake and French fries?"

I told him he could have anything he wanted. And then I asked him if I could join him for lunch.

He thought about it for a second.

"Sure," he finally said.

We had lunch together that day, at McDonald's.

And after that, we got together every Monday.

For the next 150 Mondays.

His name is Maurice, and he changed my life.

Why did I stop and go back to Maurice? It is easier for me to tell you why I ignored him in the first place. I ignored him, very simply, because he wasn't in my schedule.

You see, I am a woman whose life runs on schedules. I make appointments, I fill slots, I micromanage the clock. I bounce around from meeting to meeting, ticking things off a list. I am not merely punctual; I am fifteen minutes early for any and every engagement. This is how I live; it is who I am—but some things in life do not fit neatly into a schedule.

Rain, for example. On the day I met Maurice—September 1, 1986—a huge storm swept over the city, and I awoke to darkness and hammering rain. It was Labor Day weekend and the summer was slipping away, but I had tickets to the U.S. Open tennis tournament that afternoon—box seats, three rows from center court. I wasn't a big tennis fan, but I loved having such great seats; to me, the tickets were tangible evidence of how successful I'd become. In 1986 I was thirty-five years old and an advertising sales executive for *USA Today*, and I was very good at what I did, which was building relationships through sheer force of personality. Maybe I wasn't exactly where I wanted to be in my life—after all, I was still single, and another summer had come and gone without me finding that someone special—but by any standard I was doing pretty well. Taking clients to the Open and sitting courtside for free was just another measure of how far this girl from a working-class Long Island town had come.

But then the rains washed out the day, and by noon the Open had been postponed. I puttered around my apartment, tidied up a bit, made some calls, and read the paper until the rain finally let up in mid-afternoon. I grabbed a sweater and dashed out for a walk. I may not have had a destination, but I had a definite purpose—to enjoy the fall chill in the air and the peeking sun on my face, to get a little exercise, to say good-bye to summer. Stopping was never part of the plan.

And so, when Maurice spoke to me, I just kept going. Another thing to remember is that this was New York in the 1980s, a time when vagrants and panhandlers were as common a sight in the city as kids on bikes or moms with strollers. The nation was enjoying an economic boom, and on Wall Street new millionaires were minted every day. But the flip side was a widening gap between the rich and the poor, and nowhere was this more evident than on the streets of New York City. Whatever wealth was supposed to trickle down to the middle class did not come close to reaching the city's poorest, most desperate people, and for many of them the only recourse was living on the streets. After a while you got used to the sight of them—hard, gaunt men and sad, haunted women, wearing rags, camped on corners, sleeping on grates, asking for change. It is tough to imagine anyone could see them and not feel deeply moved by their plight. Yet they were just so prevalent that most people made an almost subconscious decision to simply look the other way—to, basically, ignore them. The problem seemed so vast, so endemic, that stopping to help a single panhandler could feel all but pointless. And so we swept past them every day, great waves of us going on with our lives and accepting that there was nothing we could really do to help.

There *had* been one homeless man I briefly came to know the winter before I met Maurice. His name was Stan, and he lived on the street off Sixth Avenue, not far from my apartment. Stan was a stocky guy in his midforties who owned a pair of wool gloves, a navy blue skullcap, old work shoes, and a few other things stuffed into plastic shopping bags, certainly not any of the simple creature comforts we take for granted—a warm blanket, for instance, or a winter coat. He slept on a subway grate, and the steam from the trains kept him alive.

One day I asked if he'd like a cup of coffee, and he answered that he would, with milk and four sugars, please. And it became part of my routine to bring him a cup of coffee on the way to work. I'd ask Stan how he was doing and I'd wish him good luck, until one morning he was gone and the grate was just a grate again, not Stan's spot. And just like that he vanished from my life, without a hint of what happened to him. I felt sad that he was no longer there and I often wondered what became of him, but I went on with my life and over time I stopped thinking about Stan. I hate to believe my compassion for him and others like him was a casual thing, but if I'm really honest with myself, I'd have to say that it was. I cared, but I didn't care enough to make a real change in my life to help. I was not some heroic do-gooder. I learned, like most New Yorkers, to tune out the nuisance.

Then came Maurice. I walked past him to the corner, onto Broadway, and, halfway to the other side in the middle of the avenue, just stopped. I stood there for a few moments, in front of cars waiting for the light to change, until a horn sounded and startled me. I turned around and hustled back to the sidewalk. I don't remember thinking about it or even making a conscious decision to turn around. I just remember doing it.

Looking back all these years later, I believe there was a strong, unseen connection that pulled me back to Maurice. It's something I call an invisible thread. It is, as the old Chinese proverb tells us, something that connects two people who are destined to meet, regardless of time and place and circumstance. Some legends call it the red string of fate; others, the thread of destiny. It is, I believe, what brought Maurice and I to the same stretch of sidewalk in a vast, teeming city—just two people out of eight million, somehow connected, somehow meant to be friends.

Look, neither of us is a superhero, nor even especially virtuous. When we met we were just two people with complicated pasts and fragile dreams. But somehow we found each other, and we became friends.

And that, you will see, made all the difference for us both.

2

THE FIRST DAY

We walked across the avenue to the McDonald's, and for the first few moments neither of us spoke. This thing we were doing—going to lunch, a couple of strangers, an adult and a child—it was weird, and we both felt it.

Finally, I said, "Hi, I'm Laura."

"I'm Maurice," he said.

We got in line and I ordered the meal he'd asked for—Big Mac, fries, thick chocolate shake—and I got the same for myself. We found a table and sat down, and Maurice tore into his food. *He's famished*, I thought. *Maybe he doesn't know when he will eat again.* It took him just a few minutes to pack it all away. When he was done, he asked where I lived. We were sitting by the side window and could see my apartment building, the Symphony, from our table, so I pointed and said, "Right there."

"Do you live in a hotel, too?" he asked.

"No," I said, "it's an apartment."

"Like the Jeffersons?"

"Oh, the TV show. Not as big. It's just a studio. Where do you live?"

He hesitated for a moment before telling me he lived at the Bryant, a welfare hotel on West 54th Street and Broadway.

I couldn't believe he lived just two blocks from my apartment. One street was all that separated our worlds.

I would later learn that the simple act of telling me where he lived was a leap of faith for Maurice. He was not in the habit of trusting adults, much less white adults. If I had thought about it I might have realized no one had ever stopped to talk to him, or asked him where he lived, or been nice to him, or bought him lunch. Why wouldn't he be suspicious of me? How could he be sure I wasn't a Social Services worker trying to take him away from his family? When he went home later and told one of his uncles some woman had taken him to McDonald's, the uncle said, "She is trying to snatch you. Stay away from her. Stay off that corner, in case she comes back."

I figured I should tell Maurice something about myself. Part of me felt that taking him to lunch was a good thing to do, but another part wasn't entirely comfortable with it. After all, he was a child and I was a stranger, and hadn't children everywhere been taught not to follow strangers? Was I crossing some line here? I imagine some will say what I did was flat-out wrong. All I can say is, in my heart, I believe it was the *only* thing I could have done in that situation. Still, I understand how people might be skeptical. So I figured if I told him something about myself, I wouldn't be such a stranger.

"I work at *USA Today*," I said.

I could tell he had no idea what that meant. I explained it was a newspaper, and that it was new, and that we were trying to be the first national newspaper in the country. I told him my job was selling advertising, which was how the newspaper paid for itself. None of this cleared things up.

"What do you do all day?" he asked.

Ah, he wanted to know my *schedule*. I ran through it for him—sales calls, meetings, working lunches, presentations, sometimes client dinners.

"Every day?"

"Yes, every day."

"Do you ever miss a day?"

"If I'm sick," I said. "But I'm rarely sick."

"But you never just not do it one day?"

"No, never. That's my job. And besides, I really like what I do."

Maurice could barely grasp what I was saying. Only later would I learn that until he got to know me, he had never known anyone with a job.

There was something else I didn't know about Maurice as I sat across from him that day. I didn't know that in the pocket of his sweatpants he had a knife.

Not a knife, actually, but a small razor-blade box cutter. He had stolen it from a Duane Reade on Broadway. It was a measure of my inability to fathom his world that I never thought for a single moment he might be carrying a weapon. The idea of a weapon in his delicate little hands was incomprehensible to me. It never dawned on me that he could even use one, much less that he might truly need one to protect himself from the violence that permeated his life.

For a good part of Maurice's childhood, the greatest harm he faced came from the man who gave him life.

Maurice's father wasn't around for very long, but in that short time he was an inordinately damaging presence—an out-of-control buzz saw you couldn't shut off. He was also named Maurice, after his own absentee dad, but when he was born no one knew how to spell it so he became Morris. It wasn't long before most people called him Lefty anyway, because, although he was right-handed, it was his left that he used to knock people out.

Morris was just five foot two, but his size only made him tougher, more aggressive, as if he had something to prove every minute of every day. In the notoriously dangerous east Brooklyn neighborhood where he lived—a one-square-mile tract known as Brownsville, birthplace of the nefarious 1940s gang Murder Inc. and later home to some of the roughest street gangs in the country—Morris was one of the most feared men of all.

As a member of the infamous Tomahawks street gang, Morris was a stick-up man, and he was brazenly good at it. He even routinely robbed people he knew. There was a dice game on Howard Avenue—fifteen or twenty people, piles of tens and twenties in a pot—and Morris sometimes liked to play. One night he announced he was robbing the game. *Ain't nobody takin' nothin' from me*, one man said. Morris hit him once in the face with the butt of his gun and knocked him out, then scooped up several hundred dollars and walked away. No one else said a word. The next day Morris leaned against a car in front of his building, smiling as the very people he had robbed walked by. He was daring them to say something. No one did.

Morris finally met his match in a spark plug named Darcella. Slender and pretty, with light skin and soft features, Darcella was one of eleven children born to Rose, a single mother from Baltimore who moved her family to the Bed-Stuy section of Brooklyn. Darcella grew up surrounded by brothers and wound up as tough as any of them; she was known to fight anyone who crossed her, male or female, throwing blizzards of punches and never seeming to tire. People weren't sure if she was crazy or just mean. In her teens she was one of the few female members of the Tomahawks, and she wore the gang's black leather jacket with pride.

Then she fell for a gang member who impressed her with his swagger. They were never a good match, Morris and Darcella. They were both too explosive, too much like each other, but they became a couple anyway. She called him Junebug, evolved from Junior, since technically he was Maurice, Jr. He called her Red, from Red Bone, a nickname for fair-skinned black women. They had three children, all before Darcella turned twenty. First came two daughters, Celeste and LaToya. And then a son—a boy she named Maurice.

Sadly for Maurice and his sisters, the language his parents understood best was a discourse of violent action, not words. Morris, in particular, was a heavy drug user and an alcoholic, and coke, dope, and Wild Irish Rose easily triggered his rages. When he came home

11

at all, it was to rail at his family with both curses and fists. He would routinely slap his daughters in the head; one time, he hit Celeste so hard he ruptured her eardrum. He would slap and push and punch Darcella with the same ruthless efficiency that terrified everyone in Brownsville, and he would slap and punch Maurice, his only son. When the boy would cry, he would say, "Shut up, punk," and hit him again.

Morris would disappear for days to be with his girlfriend, Diane, then come home and warn Darcella not to even look at another man. Morris's infidelity finally pushed her too far, and she packed up her children and found an apartment in the notorious Marcy Projects in Bed-Stuy. A complex of twenty-seven six-story buildings on nearly thirty acres, with some 1,700 apartments housing more than 4,000 people, the Marcy was riddled with drugs and violence, hardly anyone's idea of a sanctuary. But for Darcella it was a place to escape an even greater threat.

Morris found them anyway. One night he burst into their apartment and demanded to talk to Darcella. "Red, I can't let you leave me," he said, crying. "I love you." With young Maurice watching, Darcella stood her ground.

"I'm not havin' it," she said. "You're no good; get out."

Morris cocked his left fist and punched Darcella in the face.

She fell to the floor, and Maurice grabbed hold of his father's leg to stop him from hitting her again. Morris flicked the boy against a wall. That, it turned out, was a mistake: Darcella saw her son on the ground, ran to the kitchen, and came out with a steak knife.

Morris didn't flinch. It was hardly the first time he'd found himself at the point of a knife. "What you gonna do with that?" he asked.

Darcella lunged toward his chest. His arms came up to defend himself, so she stabbed him in the arms. She stabbed him again and again as he tried to block the blows, and finally he staggered into the hallway and fell, covered in blood, crying, "Red, you stabbed me! You tried to kill me! I don't believe you did this!"

Maurice, wide-eyed, watched it all. Finally, the police came and asked Morris who had attacked him so savagely.

"Some guys," is all he said.

And with that, Morris limped away. Maurice, just five years old, watched his father go. His family, as he knew it, was no more.

My first lunch with Maurice was over thirty minutes after it began, but I didn't want to say good-bye to Maurice just yet. When we stepped out into the street, the sun was bright and strong, so I asked Maurice if he wanted to take a walk in Central Park.

"Okay," he said with a shrug.

We walked into the south end of the park and strolled along a path toward the Great Lawn. Bicyclists, joggers, mothers and toddlers, laughing teenagers, everyone, it seemed, was carefree. Once again, we didn't say much; we just walked side by side. I wanted to know more about him and about the circumstances that led him to begging in the street but I held back, because I didn't want him to think I was snooping around.

I did ask him one thing.

"So, Maurice, what about you? What do you want to do when you grow up?"

"I don't know," he said without hesitation.

"No? Don't you ever think about it?"

"No," he replied flatly.

Maurice didn't spend his days dreaming of becoming a policeman, or an astronaut, or a shortstop, or the president; he didn't even know these were dreams most boys have. And even if he could have imagined a life for himself beyond the misery that was his world, what would have been the point of dreaming about that life? There was nothing Maurice wanted to be, because there was no reason to believe he could be anything except what he was—a scrounger, a beggar, a street kid.

In the park there was a brisk fall breeze, leaves fluttered away from trees, and the sun peeked through the giant elms. We seemed a million miles away from the concrete core of the city. I didn't ask Maurice any more questions. I just let him enjoy this break from his street routine. When we left the park, we passed a Häagen-Dazs, and I asked him if he wanted some ice cream.

"Can I get a chocolate cone?" he asked.

"You bet," I said.

I ordered two cones, and when I handed one to him, I saw Maurice smile for the very first time. It was not a big smile, not wide and toothy like you see with most kids. It was quick to appear and just as quick to vanish. But it happened, and I saw it, and it seemed to me like a beautiful, shiny new thing.

When we finished our ice cream I asked, "Is there anything else you want to do?"

"Can we go play video games?"

"Sure we can." So we walked to an arcade on Broadway. I gave Maurice a few quarters and watched him play StreetFighter. He lost himself in the game like any kid would. He jerked the joystick and stuck out his tongue and stood on his toes and made noises as he blew up things with his spaceship missiles. It was fun to watch him play.

Later that day, it occurred to me that buying lunch for Maurice and spending a couple of hours with him had made me feel—at very little expense in time and money—inordinately good. And that, in turn, made me feel guilty. Was the only reason I had stopped and bought him lunch to make myself feel good for a while? Had I, instead of window-shopping or going to a movie, chosen to divert myself by buying Maurice a burger and an ice cream? Was there something inherently patronizing about what I did, something maybe even exploitative?

Help out a poor kid, feel better about your own life?

I didn't have the answers back then. All I knew was that being with Maurice felt right. We left the arcade and strolled down Broadway, winding up on 56th Street, right where we had met. I opened my purse and handed Maurice my business card.

"Look, if you're ever hungry, please call me and I'll make sure you have something to eat."

Maurice took the card, looked at it, and stuffed it in his pocket.

"Thank you for my lunch and my Häagen-Dazs," he said. "I had a great day."

"Me too," I said. And then he went one way, and I went another.

I wondered if I would ever see Maurice again. Certainly there was a very good chance I wouldn't. At that time, I didn't know how tough things were for Maurice, how truly dire his family life was. If I had, I don't think I'd have let him walk away. I think I might have hugged him and never let go.

But I did walk away, and when I turned around to look for him in the bustle of Broadway, he was already gone, invisible again. I had to accept he might be out of my life for good—that our strange little friendship was over just as it was beginning.

Yet I believed then and I believe now that there is something in the universe that brings people who need each other together. There is something that helps two wildly disparate people somehow forge a bond. Maybe it is precisely the thing that haunts us most that makes us reach out to others we think can provide some solace. Maybe it was my own past that made me turn around and find Maurice that day. And maybe, just maybe, that invisible thread of fate would bring us back together again.

And then, as I walked back home, I felt a surge of regret, because, while I had given Maurice my business card, I hadn't given him a quarter for the call. This was way before cell phones, and I couldn't be sure he had a landline in his apartment. If he wanted to reach me he'd likely have to use a pay phone, which meant he would have to beg for the quarter.

But in the end it wouldn't have mattered anyway.

Because on the way home Maurice threw my business card in the trash.

3

ONE GOOD BREAK

The next day at work, I couldn't get Maurice out of my mind. I told my friend and boss, Valerie, about our lunch, and I told a couple of my fellow sales reps, Paul and Lou, about this amazing kid I'd met. Everyone had the same reaction: "That's wonderful," "Good for you," "What a great thing to do." It didn't seem like any big deal to them that day.

Of course, we were all pretty caught up in the business of advertising. When I met Maurice, I was in charge of coaxing financial companies to run ads in *USA Today*. I spent a lot of time calling my contacts at the investment firm Drexel Burnham Lambert, going after their tombstones: advertisements that formally announced a company's offering of stocks. Tombstones were boring, straightforward ads full of dry type and numbers—no photos, no pizzazz. But to us, they were Picassos—page after page of sweet commissions.

The really big prize for me was American Express. Their ad team was flirting with the idea of buying space in *USA Today*, but they weren't at all sure if we could deliver the kind of production quality they insisted on for their ads. I spent months and months cajoling them to take the plunge. I knew that getting such a prestigious account would be huge for the paper and also pretty important for me. My contacts there were two imposing, impenetrable women, and for countless meetings and lunches I felt like I was getting nowhere. But then, one afternoon, I was at my desk when one of the stoic women called: American Express was in for two pages. If they were happy with how the ad looked and where it was positioned, I was pretty sure they'd end up buying more. And they did, eventually running nearly a hundred pages of ads. That was a huge score for me, my proudest moment at *USA Today*. When I met Maurice, I was at the top of my game.

It was a long, long way from where I had come.

My dream, coming out of high school in Huntington Station, the town in Long Island where I grew up, didn't require that I get a college degree. What I really wanted to be was a stewardess. I'd been a terrible student, anyway, and the only thing I knew I wanted to do was get out of my hometown and see the world. I figured working in the airline industry was the way to make that happen.

But first, I got a job as a secretary at an insurance firm. I worked for three sweet old guys in fat ties and short-sleeve shirts, typing letters, taking dictation, answering phones. Since my office skills weren't quite up to snuff, I signed up for secretarial school, and it was there, amid the clacking Remingtons, that I met a woman who worked for Icelandic Airlines.

She told me they were hiring office staffers. Not my dream job, to be sure—I'd be at a desk instead of in the clouds—but it was a start. I made an appointment with the airline to take a typing test, and I practiced my typing night after night. When I took the test I marshaled every last bit of my focus and walked out sure I'd banged out sixty immaculate words in a minute.

I failed the test.

I was mortified, so I asked the administrator—no, pleaded—if I could walk around the block and come back and take the test again. "Please, please, I was nervous. I didn't do anywhere near my best." The administrator took pity on me and sent me around the block, and when I came back I took a deep breath and pounded the keys again.

And I failed again.

Now the administrator *really* felt sorry for me. My two failed tests gave me a chance to talk to her, to blow past the formality and be a real person, vulnerable but determined, a little goofy but a lot resourceful—and this, I would soon learn, was my strength. The administrator decided she liked me, and she recommended me for a job as a receptionist.

On the way to work on my last day at the insurance firm, driving along Northern State Parkway in my beloved beige 1964 Volkswagenn, I felt like my life, at nineteen, was finally beginning. I passed a car carrying two nuns, and they looked at me and gave me two beatific smiles. I smiled back as beatifically as I could. Then I said, "See you later, girls," and I gunned the VW. I moved from the slow lane into the fast lane, and then I felt myself lose control of the car—I'd cut across a crevice in the pavement dividing the lanes, and the car jumped just for an instant. My hands came off the wheel, and before I knew it the car was swerving toward the metal parkway divider. I got really scared, grabbed the wheel, and turned it sharply to the right. The VW spun around three times before flipping over and landing upside down on the side of the road.

And then there was silence, and broken glass was everywhere. I was lying on the inside roof of the car, staring up at the seats. I looked to my left and I saw them—the two nuns, worried looks on their faces. A businessman who pulled over after seeing the accident took off his suit jacket, laid it across the bottom of the broken driver's-side window, and pulled me out. The nuns tried to comfort me as I cried hysterically.

An ambulance took me to the hospital, and I learned that other than a couple of black eyes and losing my voice from all the crying, there was nothing wrong with me. I'd survived the crash without a scratch. I looked around for the two nuns, but they weren't there. Maybe they had been my guardian angels, cushioning me from more serious injury. Maybe God had other plans for me.

The Icelandic office was on 50th Street and Fifth Avenue, the very heart of Manhattan. Across the street from St. Patrick's Cathedral, a hundred yards from Saks Fifth Avenue, around the corner from 30 Rock—I felt like I was "That Girl," and if I'd worn a beret I'd have tossed it in the air every day. The job wasn't too exciting—I answered phones, ushered people in and out, that kind of thing—but

I still loved it because the experience was new and exciting. Eventually I got promoted to secretary and then to telephone sales, a fancy name for reservations. Most thrilling of all was that the hopelessly naïve premise of my dream—that working for an airline would somehow make me a world traveler—actually proved to be true. I got incredible discounts on plane and hotel tickets—so incredible that I'd routinely grab a girlfriend and fly to Rome on a Friday evening, spend Saturday shopping in the Trastevere district, and be back in New York City by Sunday night. Another time I got round-trip tickets to Kitzbühel, Austria, plus six nights in a classy chalet, all for fifty-seven dollars! It's hardly surprising I stayed at Icelandic for five years.

But after a while I was itching to do more, and what I saw other people doing, what I thought I could be really good at, was sales. Talking to people, building trust, schmoozing them at lunches, getting them to see things *your* way—I felt like maybe that could be my calling. The only problem at Icelandic was that the nontelephone sales staff was all male—except, of course, for Gudrun.

Gudrun was a statuesque Scandinavian beauty who was the office's token female sales rep. I figured out pretty quickly I could never hope to supplant her. Yes, I was charming and persuasive in my own nudgy way, and, sure, I was a fairly cute and certainly perky brunette. But Gudrun was tall and blonde and gorgeous and quite possibly a mythical Nordic goddess. I knew I'd hit the glacier ceiling at Icelandic, and if I wanted a career in sales I'd have to go somewhere else. I gave myself exactly six months to find a job in sales.

Then I saw an ad in the *New York Times*: "Sell Advertising Space for Twice Weekly Travel Trade Publication." I didn't have anywhere near enough experience, nor did I know anything about advertising, but I called anyway and wrangled an interview. The night before I was due in the offices of *Travel Agent* magazine, I planned to cook myself a nice dinner, shampoo and blow-dry my hair, do my nails, and get a good night's sleep—then bounce out the door the next morning and be fifteen minutes early. But plans don't always go . . . well, according to plan. As I was cutting the tips off asparagus stalks, I nearly sliced off the top of my left index finger.

I mean, the blood was *gushing*. Fortunately I had a good friend, Kim, who lived down the street, so I wrapped my finger in a towel and ran over to her apartment. She took me to the emergency room at Lenox Hill Hospital, where we sat for four hours while people with real emergencies—a gunshot wound, a cratered intestine, some sort of head trauma—were wheeled in ahead of my silly kitchen mishap. Finally it was my turn, and a doctor shot up my finger with Novocain and got out a stitching needle. I started crying so loudly he brought a nurse over to help him, and then another one, and the three of them did their best to keep me conscious while sealing up my fingertip with eight stitches. What can I say? I've been terrified of needles since I was a little girl.

When I got home just before midnight, I collapsed into bed. I hadn't eaten a thing, hadn't done my hair, hadn't painted my nails. Early the next morning I bolted out of bed, threw my hair in a ponytail, and rushed to my interview on West 46th Street. Somehow I got there at seven fifteen, just as planned. The guy interviewing me, David, came in the waiting room, took a look at my heavily bandaged finger, and asked what happened.

"Oh, I cut my finger last night."

"I hope it wasn't serious."

"No, no, not too bad."

"Did you need stitches?"

"Yeah, eight of them."

"Eight?" he said. "By God, you almost cut your finger off."

Then he looked at his watch.

"You know, this is a highly competitive business, and punctuality is extremely important. I'm impressed you got eight stitches last night and you're still fifteen minutes early."

My interview was off to a good start.

David walked me over to his desk in a big bullpen office and frowned as he looked over my résumé. "You have no sales experience," he said. "You have no advertising experience. You didn't go to college."

I'd expected to hear that, and I knew just what to say.

"Look," I told him, "I know I don't have a lot of experience. But I can tell you this. If you think *you* work hard, just watch me because I will work twice as hard as you. And if you hire me, I can promise you this: you will never, ever regret it."

And then the clincher:

"David, I'm not looking for a lot of breaks in life. But I *am* looking for *one*."

David hired me three days later. Sometimes one good break is all you need.

When I met Maurice, I'd long since buried the last of any insecurity I felt at not having a degree. I'd certainly never lied about it if anyone brought it up—"No, I never went to college," I'd say before steering the conversation elsewhere—but by 1986 this thing that had been a burden to me was now a badge of honor. I was the scrappy underdog, raised from humble roots and making her way in the world just fine.

I had a closet full of stylish Albert Nipon dresses and a silver LeBaron in the garage. I had a fabulous tan-canvas-and-brown-leather Ghurka attaché case I had paid three hundred dollars for and a Ghurka appointment book to match. I filled my cozy L-shaped studio at the Symphony with nice furniture and, every now and then, fresh flowers, and all these things—all the markers that in 1980s Manhattan defined how successful you were as a person—all these material comforts, truly and genuinely made me happy.

But they did not make me feel *fulfilled*. Even then, I had a vague sense something was missing. I was pursuing one dream—having a successful career—at the expense of everything else. I loved what I did, and I did it with passion, but my job was so consuming I didn't have time to realize what I was missing out on in life. There was almost nothing that could pull my attention away from work.

But for a couple of days after meeting Maurice, I was distracted. I made my phone calls and went to my meetings, yet found myself thinking about him a lot. I wanted to know more about him, starting with why he was on the streets begging for change.

I decided I wasn't going to wait for Maurice to call me.

I was going to go out and find him.

4

THE BIRTHDAY PRESENT

The Thursday after my lunch with Maurice, at the end of a long day at work, I went back to the corner where we met. I didn't see him at first—it was around seven thirty, the end of rush hour, and the sidewalks were still busy. But then, in the very spot where I had left him, there he was. He was wearing the same ratty burgundy sweats, the same dirty white sneakers. When he saw me coming, he smiled. This time, the smile didn't vanish so quickly.

"Hi, Maurice," I said.

"Hello, Miss Laura." I was surprised by the formality. Someone along the way had taught him to be polite.

"How are you, Maurice? Are you hungry?"

"I'm starving."

We went back to McDonald's. He ordered the same thing as

before—Big Mac, fries, thick chocolate shake—and I did, too. This time, Maurice ate more slowly. I asked him to tell me about his family.

He explained that he lived at the welfare hotel with his mother, Darcella; his grandmother Rose; and his sisters, Celeste and LaToya. This was the truth, but not the whole truth, as I would later learn. Early on, Maurice did not share all the details of his life and withheld the particularly grim ones. I thought at the time it was because he was embarrassed. Or maybe he didn't want to scare me away. If he'd wanted my sympathy, he would have told me one or two of the really bad things about his life, but he didn't. He wasn't looking for anyone's sympathy. He was only looking to survive.

"What about your father?" I asked.

"He's not around."

"What happened to him?"

"He's just gone."

"What about your mother? Does she know you're out here on the street?"

"Nah, she don't care."

I couldn't believe this was true, but then, I knew nothing about his mother's life. Maurice came and went as he pleased; no one ever asked him where he'd been or where he was going, no matter the time of day or night. He answered to no one, and, in turn, no one really looked out for him.

When I met him, Maurice had received only two gifts his entire life.

One was a little Hess truck his uncle Dark gave him when he was four.

26

The other was a present from Grandmother Rose on his sixth birthday.

"Here you go," she said, handing him a tiny white thing.

It was a joint.

Grandmother Rose was four foot eleven and hard as a two-by-four. Born in the backwoods of North Carolina, she grew up in dire poverty and learned early on how to handle adversity. She handled it by being tougher than anyone who stood in her way. Rose was pretty, with bright eyes and a curling smile, and men fought for her attention. But sooner or later they all learned the same thing: Rose took nonsense from no one. She liked to say, "I'll take you off the count," which meant she'd kill you and wipe you off the grid.

This was no idle threat: Rose always carried a sharp straight razor she nicknamed "Betsy."

Maurice liked tagging along with Rose; he liked her toughness. They were together on the subway when a man made the mistake of stepping on Rose's Timberland boots. Rose got up and pushed the man clear down the subway car, yelling, "Jack, step back, my Timberlands in the way!"

The man, overmatched, could only say, "Lady, you're crazy."

That's when Maurice, just a kid, told him, "Yo, you better shut up." He knew if the man said the wrong thing, he'd get Betsy.

Even those closest to Rose were vulnerable. One of her boyfriends, Charlie, was a tall and skinny fellow with a pretty bad stutter. Maurice got a kick out of their bickering, because Charlie's stuttered taunts just sounded silly. But then one night Charlie went too far.

"R-R-R-R-Rosa," he said. "I will m-m-m-m-mess you up."

Rose jumped at him with Betsy in her hand and sliced him from his face down to his chest. Maurice, too shocked to cower, stood there watching Charlie bleed all over the sofa.

"Y-Y-Y-You're crazy!" is all Charlie could say.

Rose told him, "You're lucky I missed the jugular."

Rose had six sons who stayed in her orbit long into adulthood, spinning away and inevitably slinking back. Maurice knew them as his uncles—a collection of men who, for better or worse, showed him how to live on the streets.

The oldest was an ex-Marine who returned from Vietnam more than a little off. Maurice enjoyed his walks with Uncle E, except when he would suddenly take off running and leave Maurice in the street. Later, Maurice would ask, "Uncle E, what happened?"

"Didn't you seem 'em?" he would say. "The Viet Cong. They was chasing me. Those slant-eyed bastards was chasing me."

Like all his brothers, Uncle E was in the drug business, but he was a minor player, a low-stakes guy. More often than not his brothers kept him away from the deals and only called on him to help with enforcement. He was good at it, not because he was especially strong or violent, but because he enjoyed cooking up schemes to isolate and punish his family's rivals. "War training," he'd say.

There was also Uncle Dark, named for his dark skin. He was the smart one, or at least smart enough to rustle up occasional work on a meat-delivery truck while also dealing cocaine during his shift. Before long, he gave up on legitimate work and threw himself full-time into dealing drugs. He had a reputation in Brooklyn as a gangster dealer: he'd sell you what you needed, but if you somehow got on his bad side, you'd quickly regret it.

Another brother was known to everyone as Uncle Limp, because he had a bad leg. When he was in prison, he'd signed up with the Five Percent Nation, a Harlem offshoot of the Nation of Islam, and he had a lot of theories about God and the devil and the role of the black man in society. Every time he went to jail, he came back with bigger and fancier words, until no one knew what he was saying. "The Asiatic black man is a personification of the esoteric powers of God," he'd announce. To Maurice, he was the uncle who made no sense.

Uncle Old, the second-oldest brother, was the meanest of the bunch. They called him Uncle Old, because he seemed like the old man of the group, in that he took care of business with ruthless authority. He was short, like Maurice's father, and he was reflexively violent—he believed boys like Maurice needed a whipping at home in order to learn how to fight on the streets. And so Maurice absorbed a torrent of smacks and punches from him. When Maurice was young, he heard rumors Uncle Old had killed several men.

Uncle Old was also the biggest and most successful drug dealer of all the uncles. When the crack epidemic hit New York City like a hurricane in the 1980s, he made his mark, buying cocaine from Dominican distributors on 145th Street and Broadway in Manhattan, then bringing it home to cook into crack and resell in Brooklyn. Sometimes he'd take young Maurice with him to pick up the drugs. Men with machine guns frisked Maurice for weapons, then held a pistol to his head while his uncle scored the drugs. Maurice, just ten, did not feel scared to have a gun trained on him. He'd learned by then that this was just procedure.

The baby of the group, just four years older than Maurice, wasn't nearly as hardened. He was the handsome one, the one the girls loved, and Maurice knew him as Uncle Nice or sometimes Uncle Cassanova. He was also one of the smarter brothers, though that didn't do him much good. As a drug dealer he was hapless and often wound up in jail. He is in federal prison today, doing ten years for drug trafficking.

And there was the aspiring hip-hopper, who gave himself the rap name Juice. Uncle Juice was terrified of police and so never joined his brothers in dealing drugs. But he smoked more marijuana than all of them combined. His fondness for pot kept him in a perpetual haze, spinning rhymes that went nowhere, like his dreams. On 9/11, Uncle Juice should have been at the World Trade Center where he sometimes worked as a freelance messenger. But that day he was too high to get in on time and, instead, watched the first plane hit the Twin Towers on TV.

"Michelle," he told his wife, "I ain't going in today 'cause a plane hit my building."

"Derek, stop playing," she said.

Uncle Juice then noticed the tower he worked in had not been hit, so he put on his clothes and got ready to go in. He was lacing up his sneakers when the second plane struck.

"Plane hit the other building," he announced, plopping on the sofa and rolling another joint. "Now I really ain't going in."

A few days later, Maurice asked him, "Uncle Juice, do you know how lucky you are?"

"Not lucky," Juice said. "I knew the planes were coming. The rats in the towers told me."

"And that," he told Maurice, by way of offering a little advice, as uncles often do, "is why you never go to work on time."

Over the years the uncles came and went. Sometimes none of them were around; sometimes only one or two; other times all six. To Maurice, they were family. They were the only family he knew.

And together with his mother and his grandmother, they were the people who cared most about him in the world. By outside standards they may not have appeared to care much about Maurice at all, but in a city that seemed hostile, in a series of welfare hotels and shelters that housed the crazy and the violent, Maurice's relatives were his only protectors. He knew whose side he was on. He knew where he was safest, if not from all harm, then at least from the worst of it.

Maurice saw that, in their own way, these people loved him. And he saw in his grandmother someone he could count on when he really needed her.

One night, when the family was staying at the squalid Prince George welfare hotel on West 28th Street in Manhattan, Maurice's mother did not come home. She did not come home the next night, either. She did not come home for two weeks. No one knew why; she was simply there one day and not there the next. Maurice's older sisters took this as a cue to fend for themselves and, though they were barely teenagers, moved in with older boyfriends. Maurice's uncles were scattered, and Grandma Rose was living in another welfare hotel, the Bryant, farther uptown.

That left Maurice all by himself at the Prince George. He was ten years old. At night he'd wander over to Park Avenue South and talk to the prostitutes who worked the streets. One of the pimps, known as Snake, took him under his wing.

"Yo, youngblood," Snake said. "I want you to do something for me."

Snake had Maurice watch as men drove by and made deals with the hookers. They'd park and take the hookers into their cars. Snake didn't want any one trick going on too long; he needed his girls on the street getting more work. So he told Maurice, "If you seen them bitches in the car for more than five minutes, go bang on the window and tell 'em police coming."

Maurice did this every night until dawn. Snake paid him in single dollar bills, and sometimes he'd finish a night with a hundred dollars.

In a way, it was Maurice's first job.

Then, as the sun came up, Maurice always spent the money the same way: he played video games for hours at a Times Square arcade.

Then one day he heard a loud knock at the door of the Prince George. It was 7:00 a.m., and Maurice had just come in from a night on the streets. He figured it was a neighbor or maybe one of his uncles, so he opened the door. Instead, he saw two white men in suits. He slammed the door and locked it; the men kept banging.

"Open up! We need to talk to you!" they yelled. Maurice went to the window and considered crawling out, but he was on the thirteenth floor. The banging got louder. Finally, Maurice hatched a plan and opened the door. "We're from the Bureau of Child Welfare," one of the men said. "We need to take you down to the lobby."

Maurice said nothing and went with the men. But he waited

for them to relax just a bit, and when they stopped in the lobby to make a call, Maurice bolted. "Stop that boy!" they yelled, barking instructions into walkie-talkies as they gave chase. Maurice ran up the block and looked back; the men had climbed into a white van and were coming after him. Maurice turned sharply and went up a block that ran against traffic so the van couldn't follow, but the van rounded the corner and kept on his tail. He ran up Fifth Avenue, again so they couldn't follow, but they managed to catch up. When they got too close he dove under a car and hid as they sped past. But when he got up, they spotted him again.

He ran past Macy's department store, past Rockefeller Center, past St. Patrick's Cathedral. Past a thousand oblivious working men and women. He made it up to 54th Street, where his grandmother was staying at the Bryant. He ran inside as the van pulled up and the men jumped out. He ran up the stairs to the fifth floor, the men close behind. He got to Grandma Rose's room and banged on the door, and when she opened it, he collapsed inside just as one of the men grabbed his arm.

"We are BCW," the man said. "This boy's mother has been incarcerated, and we need to take him with us."

Maurice's grandmother pulled out Betsy.

"My grandson ain't goin' nowhere."

The men were convinced to leave Maurice in her care.

When Maurice told me about the joint Grandma Rose gave him, he did not mention it with sarcasm or scorn. He said it matter-of-factly. To him, it had been a real gift, a true act of kindness. It meant someone had thought about him, and that was better than the alternative—to be forgotten, ignored, invisible. He didn't know there was anything wrong with being given an illegal drug. He didn't know any kind of life at all without drugs.

When he got the joint, Maurice put it to his lips, inhaled, and choked. He took another hit and coughed even more. Grandma Rose took it away from him, and from that day forward she tried her best to keep Maurice away from the scourge of drugs. She saw something in him in that moment—something different, something special. Perhaps she saw the same thing I did on that street corner.

When we both finished our McDonald's meals, Maurice and I walked toward Broadway. This time, I didn't want to just say good-bye and send him on his way.

"Maurice, how would you like to get together next Monday night and go to dinner again? We'll go to the Hard Rock Café."

"Okay," he said. "Can I wear these clothes?"

I figured they were the only clothes he owned.

"Yes, you can," I said. "So we'll meet on the same corner at seven, okay?"

"Yes, Miss Laura," he said. "Thank you for my meal."

And then he was gone, slipping into the night.

This time, I had the feeling I would see him again.

5

THE BASEBALL GLOVE

I was back on 56th Street exactly one week after I'd met Maurice, and my watch said 7:02 p.m. I felt pretty sure he'd show up, but still I didn't really know much about him and there were a million reasons he might not make it. Men in suits and women in heels hustled past, heading for drinks and dinner. At 7:05, still no sign of Maurice.

Just a few minutes later he came walking up Broadway. He still had on the burgundy sweats, but I was surprised to see they were clean. Somehow, he'd laundered them. And his face and hands, too, were scrubbed, not like the other times I'd seen him.

He'd made an effort to look his very best for dinner.

We walked up the block to the Hard Rock Café, which in those days was a happening spot. Guitars on the walls and good greasy burgers. Our waitress led us to our table; I noticed she was especially friendly and attentive toward Maurice. It was as if she understood the situation and wanted to make Maurice's night as special as I did. She handed us our menus, and Maurice disappeared behind the oversized list of appetizers and entrées.

When he emerged, he said, "Miss Laura, can I have a steak with mashed potatoes?"

"You can have anything you want."

"Okay, I'm gonna have a steak."

When a thick, sizzling slab of sirloin arrived, Maurice looked as if he'd never seen anything like it. When he picked up his giant steak knife and heavy fork, I could see he had no idea how to use them. He held the knife with his fist like a dagger. I didn't say or do anything—I didn't want to spoil his dinner with etiquette lessons. If he asked for help, then of course I would help, but for now I just let him do his thing. Finally, he tore off a piece of the steak and ate it. He must have really liked it because he smiled, and this time his smile was as wide as could be.

I was starting to really like seeing that smile.

After dinner, we walked back to our spot.

"Maurice, would you like to meet again next Monday and have dinner?" I asked.

"Yes," he said.

"So we'll meet right here, seven?"

"Okay," he said. "Thank you for my steak."

"You're welcome, Maurice. Good night now. And be careful."

He took off running, maybe back home, maybe somewhere else.

I walked to my apartment and tried not to think about where he'd gone.

The next Monday we went to the Broadway Diner on 55th Street. Maurice had passed it every day but never gone in. He'd peered through the windows once or twice, just as he'd done at dozens of other diners and restaurants and stores in Manhattan. It was just another place that wasn't accessible to him.

At the diner Maurice considered his thick menu and finally said he wanted eggs.

"Eggs?" I asked. "For dinner?"

Maurice sat there, confused. He didn't know what I was talking about. He had no comprehension of the concept of breakfast, lunch, and dinner. He didn't know different foods were served at different times. To him, there was no such thing as a structured meal.

He ate whatever he could get, whenever he got it.

Maurice ordered eggs, and when the waiter asked, "Scrambled or over easy?" Maurice guessed "over easy." He also asked for orange juice, but when it arrived he made a face and didn't touch it.

"Something wrong with your juice?"

"It's gone bad, Miss Laura," he said. "There's all this stuff floating on top."

I told him about pulp and he took a tentative sip. Then he drank his fresh juice in a couple of gulps and asked for another.

Afterward, at our spot, I said, "Maurice, next Monday? Seven?"

"Yes, Miss Laura. I'll be here. And thank you for my dinner."

By then, I was already cooking up a surprise for him, and I

planned to spring it on him the following Monday. I'd asked him if he liked sports, and he'd said he watched the Mets on TV.

"Have you ever been to a baseball game?"

"A real game? No way."

My boss at *USA Today* had season tickets to the Mets. I knew from having two younger brothers just how important and thrilling baseball could be to a boy. So that was my surprise: I was going to take Maurice to his very first baseball game.

For my younger brother, Frank, there was nothing more magical in the world, nothing more wondrous to own and to hold, than his old worn leather baseball mitt. It may have been a Rawlings, or a Wilson, I can't remember. Nor can I pretend to understand what it is about baseball and all the stuff of baseball that's so entrancing to boys. But I know that it is, and I saw it in six-year-old Frank—some elemental stirring that made him love his bat and his cap and, above all else, his glove.

I realize now, many years later, that baseball was something other than just a favorite hobby for Frank; it was his escape. We all needed one—me, my sisters, Annette and Nancy, my brothers, Frank and Steve—and we found it in different ways. For Frank, it was imagining he was batting clean-up for the Yankees. The baseball glove was his talisman: the thing he could cling to in the storm.

My family lived an outwardly typical life in Huntington Station, a solidly middle-class town an hour east of Manhattan. My father, Nunziato, was a bricklayer and a bartender, beloved by friends and neighbors and all the hundreds of people he ever gave a free drink to. Everyone called him Nunzie. He was short and stocky, with a bald spot on the top of his head, a twinkle in his eyes, and a smile that would make a stranger believe he was a friend. His hands and forearms were, to a child, cartoonishly strong. He fancied himself a builder, and he built two of the homes we lived in—plain, sturdy houses that are still there today. Most of all, my father was kinetic, restless, unable to stand still for long: he never stopped hustling, never really caught his breath.

My mother, Marie, was the opposite—a soft, retreating soul. For a time she was a waitress at a catering hall called the Huntington Town House, working long hours for little pay and handing over her checks to my father. She worked weddings, Bar Mitzvahs, anniversaries, you name it, sometimes starting at ten in the morning and not coming home until two the next morning. She was shy around new people; warm and loving with all of us. What I remember most clearly about her is how very beautiful she was. She had a lovely sweetness and innocence about her, a girlishness that would still surface whenever she found reason to be happy in her later years. I know all five of her children felt entirely loved by her; she had so much room in her heart for us that we never wanted to be anywhere else.

My father's job as a bartender meant he left for work between 6:00 and 6:30 p.m. That was pretty much the opposite of most dads, who'd be cozying up to the dinner table at about that time. As a result, we'd eat dinner at five, then watch our father leave for the night. On its own, this schedule might not have been too disruptive. After all, plenty of people work nights. But it was my father's absences—those hours after he left and before he made it home again—that most defined my childhood and that still most define the person I've become.

You see, something would happen to my father when he was away. When he came home, he was different. You could see it in the way his face had changed. You could tell by the way he parked the car. You could hear it from the sound of the car door slamming. It didn't always happen, nor was the intensity of it always the same. But it was in the waiting—in the not knowing—that the true terror resided.

One Sunday my father spent the afternoon tending bar. My mother was waitressing that day, so it was just the children at home. Around 6:00 p.m., my father came back. We scattered when we heard him pull up the driveway, all of us trying to avoid his line of sight. He went into the kitchen and there he found one of his tape measures on the table.

He picked it up. "What's this?" he said. Something was wrong with the tape measure: it was jammed. I knew Frank had been playing with it. My father had a lot of tape measures, and sometimes Frank would dig one out and fool around with it. Frank was five years old that day, two and a half years younger than me. He was a sweet, harmless kid, goofy and good-natured with an endearing stutter—an almost heartbreakingly guileless boy.

"Frank!" my father bellowed. *"Frank!!"*

My sister Annette and I sprang into action. We ran around the house shutting all the windows, so our neighbors wouldn't hear what was to come. No one had ever told us to do this; we just did it on our own out of instinct. My father trundled down the hall to my brother's bedroom and found Frank there. He stuck the tape measure in his son's face.

"What did you do to this?!"

My father never hit me or my sisters. He saved that for our mother and for poor Frank. But violence is not always a bodily thing. This time Frank flew out of the room, ahead of any blows. My father looked around the room for something to focus on.

He saw my brother's baseball mitt.

He grabbed it and stormed down the hall, through the living room, out the front door, and into the garage. Frank saw what was in his hand and chased after him, screaming, "Dad, no! I'm sorry! *I'm sorry!!*" My sisters and I followed, begging him to stop.

My father went to the wall and pulled down a pair of shearing scissors.

My father took the scissors to the glove. He ripped through the hard leather, shredding it into ragged chunks. Frank couldn't bear to see this; he ran inside the house, bawling. I went to the phone and called my mother at work: "Come home *right now*!" Annette ran and hid in her room with Nancy.

When my mother came home, she found Nunzie passed out on the living room sofa. Scattered around him: pieces of Frank's baseball mitt. Frank was curled up in a corner of his bedroom, and my mother tried to comfort him as he cried. But there was nothing she could say or do.

The next morning, my father acted as if nothing had happened. So did we. This was how we handled it, how our mother told us to handle it. I can still hear her whispering to us, "Be normal, act normal." A few days later, my father came home with a new baseball glove for Frank.

He didn't realize he could never replace the one he had destroyed.

6

IS THAT IT?

When we met on the corner on our fourth Monday together, I told Maurice that instead of going out I would cook him dinner in my apartment. He was clearly surprised, but he said, "Great." I surprised myself a little, too, with the invitation. I'd been thinking of giving Maurice a home-cooked meal, but the same doubts kept creeping in: Should I be inviting this child into my home? Could this somehow backfire? What will people think? But when I met Maurice on the corner that night—when he smiled as soon as he saw me—I knew it was okay.

We walked over to my apartment building, the Symphony. The doorman, Steve, greeted me with a wave.

"Good evening, Miss Schroff," he said.

Then he looked down at Maurice, still in his dirty burgundy

sweats. For a moment, they just stared at each other. It was Steve's job to know everyone who came and went in the building, but I could tell he was having trouble sizing up our situation.

"This is my friend, Maurice," I finally said.

That cleared up nothing.

We walked through the lobby to the elevators. The Symphony was a new building, and the spacious lobby was dazzling—gorgeous rust-and-black-granite floors, high ceilings, art deco fixtures, a grand concierge desk. Everything was sleek and shiny. The elevator was bright and roomy, and the hallway to my apartment was lushly carpeted. Maurice silently took it all in.

My apartment was small, but to me it was a luxurious sanctuary: big windows that went up to the ceiling, two double closets, a brand-new galley kitchen, and a balcony. I had a mahogany hope chest, a lovely oval dining room table, and an elegant antique bureau. The color scheme was an inviting blue and mauve. Everything was exactly how I wanted it.

I told Maurice to take a seat on the sofa. He sat up against the right arm, on the very edge of the cushion. His eyes went right to the floor where I kept my giant jug of change. It was a clear plastic jug, a couple of feet tall, filled halfway to the top with nickels and dimes and quarters. The jug idea was something I got from my father, who used to put all his bartending tips in a bucket he kept in his bedroom. He never took money out, he only put more in. We kids were fascinated to see this mountain of money grow and grow. Every March he'd sit us down and have us roll up all the coins, and it would add up to several thousand dollars, which he used to pay his taxes. Years later, when I started working, I got a big jug of my own.

I'm guessing there had to be at least a thousand dollars in coins in the jug. For a kid like Maurice, who subsisted on dimes and quarters he begged for on the street, the jug had to look like some kind of treasure.

"Do you want a Diet Coke?" I asked him.

"Yes, please," he said.

I brought out the drink and sat on the sofa.

"Maurice, I want us to have a serious conversation about something, and it's a conversation we're going to have only once, so I want you to listen carefully."

Maurice tightened up.

"The reason I invited you to my apartment is because I consider you my friend. Friendship is built on trust, and I want you to know I will never betray that trust. I want you to know you will always be able to trust me. But if you betray my trust, we can no longer be friends. Do you understand?"

Maurice looked at me with his big round eyes and said nothing. He seemed confused, even startled.

"Is that clear?" I asked again. "Does that make sense to you?"

Then Maurice asked me a question.

"Is that it? You just want to be my friend?"

"Yes, that's it."

Maurice visibly relaxed. He stood up and stuck out his hand. We shook on it.

"A deal's a deal," he said.

Much later, Maurice told me he'd been terrified when I sat him down for this talk. In his experience adults usually wanted something from him. His mother, his uncles, Snake the pimp—there was always an agenda, always an angle, to their interactions. *And now this white lady wants something too. Now,* he figured, *I'm finally going to learn why she's being so nice to me.*

It hardly made sense to him that all I wanted was to be friends.

But now we had a pact. A friendship pact. Only years later would I be able to take the full measure of what that handshake meant.

I told Maurice that while I cooked dinner I wanted him to set the table. I handed him plates and forks and knives. I put three chicken breasts in the broiler and boiled up pasta and vegetables, and I could hear Maurice fumbling with the silverware at the small table that defined my dining area. After a few minutes, he came into the kitchen.

"Miss Laura, can you teach me how to set the table?"

It was the first time he ever asked me to teach him something.

I went out and set the table as he watched. Fork on the left, knife on the right, plate, napkin, glass. When we sat down to eat, I noticed Maurice staring at my hands.

"What's the matter, Maurice?"

"I'm trying to figure out how you use your knife and fork together."

I slowed down my movements so he could see. Once again, I didn't say anything—I didn't give him a lesson. I simply let him learn by watching. Maurice was a sponge, fiercely curious and intelligent. He'd learned all the tricks of the drug trade by watching his mother and uncles; he was an expert on surviving on the streets because he'd seen it done. But he'd never seen anyone set a table or properly use a fork and a knife.

He had never eaten a meal at a dinner table in someone's home.

Now, he watched me with my knife and fork and picked it up right away. Table etiquette isn't a crucial skill in life, but it is a handy one. And Maurice, I could tell, was more than eager to learn it.

I noticed Maurice ate only half his dinner.

"Is your chicken okay?" I asked.

"It's great," he said.

"How come you didn't finish it? Aren't you hungry?"

Maurice looked sheepish.

"I want to bring some home to my mama," he said. "Is that okay?"

"Maurice, I have more in the kitchen. You finish that, and I'll make you a plate you can take home."

Maurice devoured the rest of his dinner.

Afterward, we both cleared the table, and in the kitchen I handed him a roll of cookie dough.

"How about some cookies? You cut 'em; I'll bake 'em."

I gave him a knife; he wasn't sure what to do. I showed him how to open the roll and told him to cut each piece about an inch thick and then into four more pieces. Maurice listened and went to work. We arranged the pieces on a cookie sheet, put them in the oven, and, fifteen minutes later, ate warm chocolate chip cookies with milk.

Maurice *loved* the idea of dessert—it was something else he wasn't used to having. It was a treat, and he didn't have many treats in his life. It became his favorite part of our meals together. He made sure to tuck away four cookies to bring home.

It was nearly 9:00 p.m., and I wanted to get Maurice home. I still couldn't believe no one would wonder where he'd been. I wrapped up a plate of food for him, and we sat down to talk before he left.

"Maurice, let me ask you something. Do you have your own toothbrush at home?"

"No," he said.

"Do you have a towel or a washcloth?"

"No."

"Do you have a bar of soap there?"

"No, Miss Laura."

I went to my closet and pulled out a towel and a washcloth, and I found an extra toothbrush and toothpaste and a bar of soap. I put them in a plastic shopping bag along with the leftovers. I would soon learn that anything Maurice brought home with him quickly disappeared. His sisters, his uncles, he didn't know who took them exactly—the stuff just vanished. Eventually I bought Maurice a large footlocker with a combination lock, and he kept his stuff in there.

"One more thing," I said to Maurice. "I have a surprise for you."

He perked up.

"How would you like to go to a Mets game this Saturday?"

Maurice lit up. All these years later, I can still see his face in that moment, bathed in something like joy.

"But listen, Maurice. I need your mother to sign a note saying she's okay with you riding in my car and going to the game, okay? Can you bring this to her and have her sign it?"

I'd typed up a permission slip and gave it to him. I asked him to meet me on Wednesday, same time and spot, with the note. "I'm not going to take you to the game without it," I told him. "You must get this signed and bring it back." He promised he would, and we agreed to meet that Wednesday so he could give me the note.

"Thank you so much for my dinner and all this stuff," Maurice said.

I walked him down through the lobby and past Steve again.

"Good night, Maurice," Steve said.

Maurice was startled. The doorman knew his name.

That Wednesday night I waited on 56th Street for Maurice to bring me the note. I waited for ten minutes, then fifteen, then twenty. I waited until seven forty-five.

Maurice never showed up.

7

A MOTHER'S SONG

During one of my early dinners with Maurice—I can't remember which—I asked him to tell me more about his mother. He was hesitant to say anything about her at all, but I pressed him a bit. I felt I needed to know as much about her as I could. After all, I was spending time with her son, infringing on her territory. Could his mother really not care what he did or who he was with?

"Maurice, does your mother work?" I asked.

"No."

"So what does she do all day?"

"She stays home and she cleans. She vacuums and dusts."

This made sense to me; plenty of moms are stay-at-home moms. I formed a picture of Maurice's mother in my mind: harried, exhausted, too many kids, no man to help. I was still trying to get my head around how a boy his age could be on his own to roam the streets at night. What mother would allow that? And if she did, why hadn't Maurice shown up that Wednesday? Had she not wanted him to go to the Mets game with me? Was his mother even in his life anymore?

After Maurice didn't show up with the note, I decided I had to find out these things for myself. I decided to go to the Bryant Hotel and meet Maurice's mother.

All I knew was what Maurice had told me: that he lived with his mother and grandmother and sisters in a room at the Bryant. I knew it was a welfare hotel. In the news, I'd heard a bit about New York City's many welfare hotels, but I'd never been to one, or even near one. I figured it would be better if I didn't go alone, so I asked my friend Lisa, who lived three doors down the hall from me, to come along. After work on Thursday we walked over to the Bryant, on the corner of 54th Street and Broadway.

The Bryant was in a busy but run-down stretch of midtown Manhattan, just a few blocks up from Times Square. It was a squat twelve-story building, with a limestone façade giving way to a corroded brick exterior. Down the block was the Ed Sullivan Theater that today houses the David Letterman show but in those days was where they taped the CBS sitcom *Kate & Allie*. Maurice would later tell me the sitcom helped him survive. He would go into the theater during tapings and sit in the audience, then go backstage and eat food set out on tables for the crew. After a while people assumed the boom guy, a tall black man, was his dad. The crew got to know him and let him hang around, but then the show went off the air. It was a good ride while it lasted.

Lisa and I walked up to the entrance of the Bryant. On the sidewalk outside, men and women milled around talking and yelling and laughing, and several children played and chased one another around parked cars. They were about Maurice's age and I looked to see if he was there, but he wasn't. We walked up three concrete steps and through the front door into the Bryant's wide lobby, and there, too, life was spilling over: old women and young children and loud men—a noisy, chaotic scene. The lobby reeked of something: a stale, dirty smell. The walls were painted a glossy beige, and whatever furniture had once been there was long gone. The floors were grimy and littered with newspapers and coffee cups. Two overhead fluorescent bars lit the lobby with an eerie, flickering glow.

On one side, a uniformed guard sat in a small Plexiglas booth. He looked us over as we walked in and slid open a partition so he could hear us.

"We are friends of Maurice Mazyck," I said. "We'd like to go up and see him."

"Maurice, the little kid?" he said. "You know him?"

"Yes, we're friends of his."

The guard looked suspicious, but he came out of his booth and walked us to the elevators. The main elevator, with a crudely painted black door covered with scrawled graffiti, wasn't working. The guard took us a little farther back to the freight elevator. He rang a buzzer, and another uniformed guard arrived to take us upstairs. The freight elevator rattled up to the fifth floor. The hallway was dark and dreary: no carpet, crumbling plaster walls, scattered trash, a strong smell of fried food. The baseboards were black with soot. Everything was strangely quiet, compared to the lobby. Save for a distant raised voice, it seemed all but abandoned. We came to apartment 502, marked only by two numbered stickers—the 5 was missing—and the guard stood behind us, watching. I looked at Lisa, and her face told me she was thinking the same thing I was—we had crossed over into a world neither of us knew existed. I took a deep breath and knocked on the door of 502.

For a long time, nothing happened. No one stirred inside. I knocked again—still nothing.

"Go ahead. Knock again," the guard said.

Finally, I heard a sound inside the apartment: shuffling footsteps coming to the door. A lock turned slowly, then another. The door creaked open.

A woman appeared and leaned against the doorframe. She had on brown sweatpants with no drawstring; the pants were sliding down past her underwear. She had on a stained white T-shirt and nothing on her feet. Her dark hair was matted and wild. Some of it covered her face; some of it stuck straight up. I couldn't tell how old she was. She might have been eighteen or forty. She was bone-thin, and her movements were in slow motion. Her knees seemed close to buckling. She looked in our direction, but I could see she did not register our presence. She was in some kind of trance, awake but not really conscious. She opened her mouth as if to say something, but only a slurred, mumbled sound came out. She propped her head against the door frame. Her eyes rolled back in her head.

This was Maurice's mother, Darcella.

There were many, many nights in Brooklyn when Darcella did not know where she and her children would sleep. The girls, Celeste and LaToya, weren't even ten yet, and Maurice was a tiny wisp of a thing, barely six. Their father, Morris, had just disappeared for good, so they were on their own. Some nights they stayed in shelters; some nights, with a cousin. Some nights Darcella would bring the children with her to a friend's house to do drugs, and she'd pass out there. Maurice and his sisters would huddle together in a corner and sleep until morning came.

Some nights, the family would be rousted from wherever they were staying and sent into the streets. Maybe they'd overstayed their welcome in a cousin's apartment; maybe there had been a fight at a shelter. Darcella would walk with her children down desolate streets, heading nowhere, and sing to them so they would feel less afraid. She had a beautiful voice; when she was younger she had sung in a church choir. Maurice loved hearing her sing. He liked when she sang uplifting gospel hymns, but most of all Maurice loved it when his mother made up songs on the spot. She'd point out something on the street and work it into a lyric: an abandoned car, a stray cat, a junkie in an alley. And the sweet, lilting chorus was always the same:

> *How can this be*
> *Me and my three*
> *Living so desperately*

If they were lucky, they found a shelter to take them in for the night.

Darcella—uncommonly pretty, with dimples that sprang up whenever she smiled—began doing drugs shortly after Maurice was born. By then, everyone in her life was already an addict: her husband, her many brothers, even her mother. The places she lived were havens for dealers and drug fiends. It was as if a relentless tide finally swept her under. When Maurice was an infant, she became addicted to heroin.

The addiction consumed her whole. She shot heroin into her veins right in front of her children. Young Maurice watched her drug ritual without understanding what it meant. All he knew was that when it was over, his mother was happy, and so it did not seem to him to be a hideous thing. He'd watch as Darcella gathered her works: the cap to a ketchup bottle, a syringe, a thick rubber band, a strip of tin foil, a cotton ball, a lighter, and a glassine packet of heroin. He'd watch as she filled the cap with water and gripped it with a pair of pliers. Then the heroin went in and on top of it a cotton ball that absorbed the dope. Then the lighter beneath the cap, heating it all up. She'd roll up the cotton ball and stick the syringe into it, drawing the heroin into the needle. Then she'd wrap the rubber band around her arm and pull it tight until a vein popped up and then press the needle into the vein and push down. Toward the end of a stash of heroin, after she'd shot up many times, she wouldn't be able to find a vein in her arm, so she'd shoot herself in a branch of the ulnar artery in her hand, between the index and middle fingers.

As she injected, she'd say, "Oh, that's good," and her head would tilt back. She would hum a tune and wave her hand through the air to the melody, and she would drift, drift, drift away until there was no pain at all.

For Maurice, these were the best moments—when his mother found her peace. It was the moments that came before it, when she was fidgety, angry, hopelessly restless, that upset Maurice and made him want to help his mother somehow. It happened once on the subway, the agitation and restlessness, and Darcella pulled out her works right there, right in front of everyone.

"Stand up around me," she told her children, and Maurice and his sisters formed a wall so no one could see her shoot up. A minute later it was over, and the children sat down. Darcella was drifting and people were staring, but Maurice didn't care, because his mother was happy now and that's all that mattered to him.

Maurice did not understand what his mother was doing to herself, nor did he comprehend what she did to pay for her habit. All he knew was that men would come into their apartment—strange men—and leave a short while later. Sometimes, though, the men would never make it past the doorway. Sometimes they walked straight into a trap.

When they were living in the dangerous Marcy Projects in Bed-Stuy, Darcella often lured men to her apartment and gave them sex in exchange for money or drugs. But, more often than not, the promise of sex was just a ruse. Usually this happened late at night, while Maurice and his sisters were asleep on the tiger-striped living room sofa, but sometimes Maurice would be awake and watch it all go down. His uncle Juice, then sixteen, would stand behind the door holding a ten-pound dumbbell. He'd wait until Darcella brought the man inside, then jump out and hit the man on the head with the weight. They'd rifle through his pockets and take everything. Then Uncle Juice would drag him down to the lobby and leave him there. One time Juice didn't even bother going to the lobby; he cold-cocked his victim, pushed him into the hallway, and left him there.

A short while later, cops knocked on the door and asked Darcella if she knew the man on the floor outside her apartment. She shrugged and said no, closed the door, came inside, and shot up the heroin she'd stolen.

Another night Maurice was awakened by screams. Uncle Juice had clocked a john, but he hadn't hit him square and the man was still conscious—dazed and bleeding, but conscious. The man ran into the apartment, right past Maurice, screaming for help with Juice on his heels. The man ran into the bathroom, and Juice followed. There were loud bangs and more screams, and Maurice, terrified but curious, came around and peeked into the bathroom. He saw the man wedged between the tub and the toilet, trying to shield himself from Juice's blows. The man was begging, pleading, cowering, and Darcella came in and said, "Give up the money." Finally the man threw out a few crumpled bills. Darcella scooped them up, looked them over, and said, "How you think you gonna get anything with this?" Uncle Juice tried to find an angle to hit the man flush, and the man pleaded again for his life. Maurice saw then, for the first time, the cold, cold face of fear in a grown man, and it chilled him to the bone. When Grandma Rose finally came into the bathroom, he felt relief, because she would stop the assault and send the poor man on his way. The man seemed to sense this, too, and said to Rose, "Please, please, help me, please."

Rose told Juice, "Club him and get him out of here. We tryin' to sleep."

Juice hit the man again, and the man finally gave in. They fleeced him and dragged him out, closing the door behind him.

Other times, it wasn't strange men who came to the apartment;

it was the police: loud banging on the door and three or four uniformed cops coming in, grabbing Darcella by the arms and dragging her away handcuffed while Maurice and his sisters yelled for them to let her go, let her go. Darcella would come back later that day and disappear into a brand-new batch of heroin. Many years later Maurice learned his mother was a part-time informant for the NYPD. She'd rat out drug dealers at the Marcy Projects, and in exchange the cops would cut off a bit of the heroin they confiscated and let her keep it. When they wanted to talk to her, they'd come and arrest her, so her cover wouldn't be blown.

But then Darcella vanished for a week. She finally returned in a wheelchair, both legs in full-length casts. She told Maurice she'd been in a car accident, and he believed her. Until he started hearing whispers on the streets. The projects talk, and Maurice learned a drug dealer had discovered his mother was a snitch and broken both her legs. Maurice asked his uncles about it; they told him to shut up.

Drugs were a part of Maurice's life as far back as his memory goes and even farther. Drugs nearly killed him when he was just one. After his birth in Kings County Hospital on Clarkson Avenue in Brooklyn, Maurice and his family moved in with his mother's older sister, Belinda, in a run-down two-story house. Young Maurice liked to sleep in his aunt's bed in her second-floor room, and most nights that was fine with her. But some nights Aunt Belinda got high on cocaine, and if she smoked too much coke, she'd have Maurice stay with his mother on the first floor.

On one of those nights, not long after shooing Maurice away, Aunt Belinda accidentally lit her bed on fire. Her boyfriend tried to douse it, but he used alcohol instead of water and only made it worse. Firemen came and put out the blaze, but by then Aunt Belinda had burned to death. The bed where Maurice normally slept was a charred black pile of ash.

Between that fire and the time I met him, Maurice lived in at least twenty different apartments, shelters, or welfare hotels. He'd moved more often than most people do in a lifetime, often after just a day or two in one place. For a while his family lived in the Van Dyke Houses, a public housing complex in Brownsville known then and now for its rampant crime and drugs. From there they moved to the infamous Marcy Projects, a similarly sprawling collection of neglected buildings and concrete courtyards.

The next stop was an Emergency Assistance Unit—a temporary shelter for families on their way to other, more permanent housing. After a short stay there, they were on to the Roberto Clemente shelter in the Bronx, six hundred cots in the middle of a warehouse and two bathrooms. Maurice had his own cot, but not for long: some clothing was stolen, Darcella confronted some people, and a fight broke out. After just three days it was back to the EAU.

From there they moved to a shelter on Forbell Street, on the border of Queens and Brooklyn. This one was better—eight or nine rooms with twenty cots in each. A modest cafeteria, even a small rec room for kids. But the Fordell was not permanent housing, so after five months it was time to move again. A series of seedy, dangerous welfare hotels came next: the Bullshippers Lodge in Brooklyn, a motel by the airport in Queens, a nameless place on Washington Avenue—filthy, dreary rooms with mirrors on the ceiling and mice crawling up the walls. Between families some of the rooms were used by hookers; on the way in Maurice would often find semen or condoms on the sheets. After a few days it was back to Fordell, before being shipped out again.

Finally, the family was back at EAU. But since they'd been in the system so long, they were given a take-it-or-leave-it choice. It was either the Brooklyn Arms or the streets. The Brooklyn Arms, Maurice had heard people say, was the worst of New York City's sixty notorious welfare hotels. You'll get mugged there. You could get killed there. Destitute people often chose the streets over the Brooklyn Arms, feeling they'd be safer. And now Maurice was on his way there—the very worst place he could imagine.

Maurice was ten when he moved into room 305 at the Brooklyn Arms. A grand, gothic sixteen-story building on Ashland Avenue, it was once known as the Granada, a posh residential hotel where wealthy families held weddings in the Forsythia Room and old ladies in white gloves had afternoon highballs. But by the 1970s, the prosperous tenants were gone and the Granada became the Brooklyn Arms.

The hallways were slathered with oily brown paint, the water and electricity came and went, the rats were nearly as big as cats. The rooms had no kitchens, but many tenants set up makeshift cooking areas—skillets, hot plates, coffee pots—that posed a terrible safety risk. Any number of neglected conditions—faulty wiring, crumbling stairwells, drug deals gone wrong—could prove deadly at any instant.

"Unless God spares them," New York senator Patrick Moynihan said in a speech denouncing the hotel, "children are going to die there."

He would be proven right: in the mid-'80s two boys—friends of Maurice's—tumbled to their deaths down a shaft while playing near a broken elevator door.

Maurice moved into 305 with his mother, his grandmother, his two sisters, and, at varying times, his six uncles. Another man, Uncle Cheese—his aunt's boyfriend—lived there, too. Sometimes as many as ten people were crammed in a single room. Maurice's time there coincided with the advent of crack in New York City; between 1984 and 1990, the use of crack in the United States became a full-blown epidemic. A form of cocaine that could be smoked, crack was highly addictive, which meant greater demand, which meant more crime and violence. It was during the crack epidemic that the homicide rate for young black men in the United States more than doubled. Countless lives were laid waste, countless children stripped of their childhoods and shunted into foster care. In some ways, welfare hotels like the Brooklyn Arms were ground zero in the epidemic. It was there that crack was bought and sold, cooked and smoked, swallowing families whole.

Ironically, crack hit the Brooklyn Arms at a time when Maurice's mother was desperately trying to get clean. Not long after they moved there, she checked into an in-patient rehab center at Kings County Hospital. She stayed there for three months, ridding her body of poisons. Maurice cried every night while she was away. Finally, Uncle Dark couldn't take the crying anymore, so he rounded up Maurice and his sisters and took them to the hospital to see their mother. They got there long after visiting hours were over, and a guard refused to let them in. Uncle Dark said, "I ain't come up here for nothin'," so he walked around the perimeter of the hospital yelling for Darcella.

"Dee Dee!" he hollered. "Dee Dee, where you at?!"

Soon Maurice was yelling too: "Mommy, Mommy, it's me!"

They walked and yelled and finally heard a faint voice: "I'm over here." Maurice saw his mother looking out a second-floor window. She was crying and saying, "My babies! My babies!" Darcella reached out her arms as if to grab her children from two stories up, and Maurice held out his arms as if to let her scoop him up. Finally she said, "You better get out of here before I get in trouble."

But Maurice refused to go; he cried and rolled on the ground and said, "I'm not leaving." Uncle Dark slung Maurice over his shoulder and carried him away, the boy's cries cutting through the night, bringing patients to their windows as Darcella disappeared inside.

She made it home a few weeks later, clean for the first time in years. Maurice didn't understand what rehab was, but he could see his mother was different, better, happier. She would spend more time with Maurice and his sisters; she'd ignore all the uncles as they came and went with their drugs. For the first time in his life, Maurice had a mother who wasn't strung out all the time. For the first time he experienced something close to normalcy. The Brooklyn Arms, it turned out, wasn't such a bad place after all.

Until one day when Uncle Dark came home and said, "Yo, Dee Dee, come here. I want you to try somethin'. This is something different."

"No, man, I'm done," she told him.

"Yo, Dee, this ain't nothin' like the old stuff. This is freebase."

"I don't care, I don't care. I'm done."

Uncle Dark laid a rock of crack on the table.

"Yo, Dee, you gotta try this high, you don't know what you missing. And Dee, *this shit don't get you hooked*."

Darcella stared at the rock for a long time. Finally she took it into the bathroom. She came out a minute later, and her eyes were watery. They were open as wide as fifty-cent pieces. Maurice was still too young to realize what exactly had happened, but he was old enough to think, *This is not good*.

And just like that Darcella fell off the razor's edge separating one world from another and tumbled permanently to the dark side.

Room 305 became the crack headquarters of the Brooklyn Arms. Once Darcella got a taste for the drug, she became the biggest crack dealer in the hotel—bigger than any of the uncles. She was the first one to learn how to cook cocaine and turn it into crack; she taught her brothers how to do it, too. The uncles would buy coke from the Dominicans on upper Broadway and bring it home for Darcella to cook. Sometimes she went out and bought the drugs herself. Money poured in like never before, wads and wads of bills.

Years later, Maurice guessed that in less than a year, with his mother and his uncles all dealing at once, at least a million dollars in cash passed through his apartment at the Brooklyn Arms.

And all that money brought its own sense of stability: for the first time, Darcella had enough to buy her children shoes and coats and underwear. People treated his mother and uncles with respect, and that trickled down to Maurice, who felt important, too. Life had a rhythm to it, a predictable chaos. Maurice believed that, finally, he had a place he could call home.

And then, the Brooklyn Arms erupted in flames.

In 1986 two children started a fire in their room. Their mother wasn't home; she was out copping drugs. The children, too scared to run and too young to know better, hid in a closet. Smoke was everywhere. People were running and screaming. Maurice stood on the sidewalk and watched children—children he knew—stagger out stiff-armed and burned and crying. In all, four children died in the fire.

Afterward, Mayor Ed Koch denounced conditions at the hotel and pledged to clean it up. Not much later, police raided the Brooklyn Arms. They banged on doors and slapped handcuffs on tenants. Maurice's mother happened to be walking down the stairs at the very instant police were charging up. She convinced cops she was just a drug addict, only there to score, and not a dealer who sold drugs out of her room. The police let her walk, but two of Maurice's uncles were arrested in the raid. Once again, Maurice stood on the sidewalk, watching police and camera crews swarm the place he called home. He watched the news crews leave that night, and he watched the dealers go back to dealing the minute they were gone.

Just a few days after the raid, his uncle Limp got drunk and threw a brick through the laundry room window, and Maurice and his family were kicked out of the Brooklyn Arms for good.

At the Bryant, I looked past Darcella as she slumped against the door frame, into the room where Maurice lived. It was about twelve square feet, with two windows and a high ceiling. Toward the back there were two single beds with no sheets or pillows. There was a beat-up, beige La-Z-Boy chair and a half-sized refrigerator with a small TV balanced on top. Maurice would later tell me the fridge never—not once—had any food in it. All he ever found there were a plastic jug of water and a box of baking soda used for cooking drugs.

That was it; there was nothing else in the room. It was dark and bare: no pictures on the walls, dim overhead lighting, no curtains, no kitchen. I saw an older woman sitting in the chair—this was Rose. I couldn't see anyone else, but I would soon learn Maurice lived in that room with as many as twelve people—his mother and grand-mother, his sisters, an aunt and her two young children, one uncle full-time, and two or three more uncles coming in and out. The five young children slept in the single beds at night while the adults stayed up and did drugs. When morning came, the children got up and the adults crashed and slept away the day. Sometimes the uncles would sleep on the floor, sometimes in the room's one closet.

Sometimes Maurice would take the closet for himself to get some privacy.

"Hello, I'm Laura," I finally said. "I'm friends with Maurice. Are you his mother?"

The woman stared at us blankly, absorbing nothing.

"Did Maurice mention the baseball game to you? I want to take him to a Mets game, and I need your permission, if that's okay."

The woman slid farther down the door frame. Her eyes rolled farther back in her head. I had seen people too drunk to stand or too high to talk, but I had never, ever seen anyone as out of it as this. Finally, she steadied herself, turned, and slowly shuffled away. The security guard began moving toward the elevator.

Then Grandma Rose came to the door. She was much more alert, and she looked us over and frowned and said, "What's this?"

"Hi, my name is Laura, and this is my friend Lisa. I'm friends with Maurice. I don't know if he's told you about me."

"He has," Rose said.

"Oh, okay. That's good. Well, I want to take Maurice to a Mets game this weekend, and I need to get his mother's permission."

I handed Rose the note and a pen. She took the piece of paper, signed her name. She said, "That's fine," and handed it back.

"Thank you so much," I said. "And can you tell Maurice to stop by my apartment when he gets the chance?"

Rose said, "Yes," and closed the door.

The next day my intercom buzzed, and Steve the doorman told me Maurice was downstairs.

"Send him up," I said.

Maurice came in with a serious look on his face. "Miss Laura," he said, "you have to promise you'll never go to that place again."

I told Maurice I had to go to get his mother's permission.

"You have to promise me you'll never go back there again."

"Maurice, it's okay."

"No, it's not. Nice white ladies should never be in a place like that. You can't go back there. Promise me you won't go back there."

I promised him that I wouldn't, and I never did.

At the time I thought Maurice was merely embarrassed by his living situation, but as I learned more about his family, I realized he was protecting me. He knew what his uncles were capable of; he knew how quickly someone could be victimized. Maurice never told a single relative where I lived or all that much about me.

He did not want me to even brush up against his world.

That Saturday Maurice met me in the lobby of the Symphony, and we went to the garage to get my car and drive the twenty minutes up the Grand Central Parkway to Shea Stadium. Maurice was beyond excited; he was bouncing in the front seat. I'd asked my boss, Valerie, for the tickets, and she'd been nice enough to let me have them. They were unbelievable seats—a few rows behind first base. We walked through the concourse and into a tunnel. As the tunnel opened up and revealed the impossibly green grass of the infield, I looked at Maurice and saw his mouth fall open. It's one thing to watch a game on a tiny black-and-white TV set. It's another to see the ballplayers up close, playing catch in their bright white uniforms, hitting balls with a crisp crack of the bat. Like I said, baseball doesn't mean much to me, but to boys it does. And to Maurice it was a little bit of heaven, a bigger thrill than he could have imagined. I don't remember seeing him blink even once over the next three hours. He watched the game and ate hot dogs and sipped a soda and cheered the players, and, like every other kid in the park, he lost himself in the unfolding story of a simple baseball game.

I can't say if that was one of the happiest moments in Maurice's young life, but I do know it was one of the happiest moments in mine.

8

A FATHER'S LEGACY

What does it mean when society says you're unfit to be a mother? Are there circumstances to be factored in before that judgment is made? What if a mother is doing the best she can in the face of crushing adversity but still doesn't measure up to society's standards?

When does a mother lose her right to be a mother?

There is a story of a young mother named Maria Giuseppe Benedetto, who was left alone to raise six children when her husband, Pasquale, was drafted into the Italian army in 1914. Maria and Pasquale lived in the southern Italian town of Gioia del Colle, one of the poorest regions in the country. The men were mostly farmers, like Pasquale, struggling against constant droughts and harsh terrain. Still, they tilled the same parched land their ancestors tilled, and they kept their families going as best they could.

But when Pasquale was called to military service at the start of World War I, his family faced catastrophe. Maria and her children—the eldest was thirteen—were left with no source of food or income save for the barren land. They scavenged the fields for anything edible, scrounging stray dandelions or anything else that could help make a meal. Pasquale was allowed to come home some weekends and help his eldest son, Pietro, work the farm, but the long winter months passed slowly. Maria lay awake on cold nights worrying her children would starve.

Then, during one of Pasquale's visits, Maria became pregnant with their seventh child. Now she needed her husband more than ever. When she was in her eighth month, in early 1917, she hitched up a horse and wagon, left Pietro in charge of the others, and took the long trip to military headquarters in the town of Bari. There, she sought out the commanding officer, barged into his office, and demanded her husband be discharged. *He has six hungry children at home*, she told him. *He belongs with his family.* The officer felt pity but could do nothing to help. The best he had to offer was a promise to keep Pasquale away from the front lines so he'd be safe until the war was over.

Maria, distraught and exhausted, steered the horse back to Gioia del Colle on rutted dirt roads. Along the way, she felt a great pain in her stomach. She made it home just in time to give birth to her seventh child, Annunziata. Now things were tougher than ever—but they would get even worse. In Bari, Pasquale's commander broke his promise and shipped him to the Italian front in Gorizia, where the army sought to seize Austrian land along the Isonzo River. Nine times before, the army had tried securing this territory, and all nine times they had failed. The tenth campaign fared no better.

Two months after giving birth, Maria got word Pasquale had been shot and killed in action.

Now that she was a widow with seven young children, the local authorities finally took notice and stepped in. What they decided to do was declare Maria unfit to care for all of her children and take two of them away.

Young Luca was sent to a state school for boys, while Giustina was packed away to the Instituto Femminile di Maria Cristina di Savoia—a boarding school run by nuns. They were kept there, away from their family, for several years. Maria was allowed to visit them once a month.

And then, in the summer of 1917, Maria's mother fell ill. Maria left Pietro in charge of his sisters Rosa and Ana and his brother Donato while she trudged to her mother's home in the nearby hills, her infant in tow. One day, after finishing their chores, the children were playing in the field, skipping and running and throwing sticks, when young Ana, then five, came upon the family's well. It was a hole in the ground surrounded by slabs of white rock with a larger white stone moved on and off to seal the hole. Maria, in her haste, had left the big stone off. And now young Ana tried to tiptoe around the edge of the well, just for fun.

She tripped and fell, tumbling down the hole.

Rosa ran one mile to her grandmother's house to get help, but it was too late. The child drowned at the bottom of the well.

Local authorities investigated the incident and deemed Maria unfit to handle her family. Now young Rosa, not yet eight, was sent away to the Maria Cristina di Savoia.

Society had come up with a solution to Maria's problems. The solution was to take her children away.

But there was nothing Maria could do, and she found some solace in knowing her daughters were enjoying their time at the school. Still, Maria could not get over the pain of losing her family. She vowed that one day she would bring all her children together again, and she wrote to her brother Pietro who, with the help of her brother-in-law, had emigrated to America. She asked them for help in moving her family there, too. They sent her enough money to make the trip to America, Maria pulled her children from their schools, and, in January 1921, boarded a boat called the *Duca D'Aosta* docked at a port in Naples. The boat met hellacious storms in the Atlantic, and a sailor had to save Rosa from being hurled overboard.

On February 19, 1921, the *Duca D'Aosta* docked at Ellis Island in the shadow of the Statue of Liberty, and Maria and her family set foot on American soil. They were quarantined on the island for several weeks because Annunziata had measles, but eventually they were free to go. They took a clanking subway ride uptown and moved into a cramped tenement apartment on East 112th Street with barely enough room for all of them. However, it had a sink, a stove, an icebox, and indoor plumbing—things they'd never had before. They lived their lives in America, with all of its glories and hardships, and their children's children lived good lives, too, and even their children, and even theirs.

I know this to be true, because Maria Giuseppe Benedetto was my great-grandmother.

Little Rosa, one of the daughters taken from Maria—and who she took back—was my grandmother. I've heard stories about how playful and clever Rosa was. When she was young, she was put in charge of cleaning the supper dishes. She watched the family dog lick his plate clean and got an idea. One by one, Rosa gave the dinner plates to the dog until he licked them all clean. Her mother was impressed with how quickly and thoroughly she'd done her chore—and she'd have gotten away with it if her sister Annunziata hadn't ratted her out.

In elementary school Rosa discovered she had a beautiful singing voice. She sang in the church choir, and the family even saved enough money to buy a secondhand piano for her lessons. But the joy she took from singing would not last long. In her teens she met a man named Sebastiano Vito Procino—dark, handsome, and ten years older than her. Sebastiano's life, from an early age, was one of hard, uncompromising work. When he was an eight-year-old boy growing up on a farm in Gioia del Colle—the same poor town where Rosa was raised—he was taken out of school and sent into the fields to shepherd a large flock of sheep. That meant rising before dawn, packing some food, and tending to the sheep as they grazed on the hillside for twelve hours. He spent his days alone, with only the sheep for company.

This experience shaped the person he became. After serving in the elite Bersaglieri Corps in the Italian army for five years and coming to America in 1923, Sebastiano worked as a laborer for the Erie Lackawana Railroad, and then as a building supervisor, and then as a skilled plasterer—demanding, backbreaking jobs. The guiding principle of his life was to provide for the family he started with Rosa—seven children in all—and to instill in them the value of hard work and sacrifice. To Sebastiano, being a man meant always being vigilant, never being soft, and refusing to tolerate anything frivolous.

One thing Sebastiano could not tolerate was singing.

Sebastiano forbade his wife from singing in a choir or anywhere else. He believed her beautiful voice made her more attractive to other men, and so, the dutiful wife that she was, she never sang in public again. I would like to think that in private moments my grandmother sang her heart out, away from her husband's ears, but I do not know for sure that she did.

Another frivolous thing for Sebastiano was affection.

Sebastiano was not a tyrannical father; some Sunday mornings he'd take his children to the bakery for fresh rolls and walnut rings, and in the summer he drove them to Carvel for ice cream. But he had been raised by an abusive father who showed him no affection, and he did not believe a parent should ever show any feelings for his children. Being demonstrative was a sign of weakness, and Sebastiano was anything but weak. He believed children should be raised not with love but with discipline and, if warranted, physical punishment.

At suppers, he kept a strap across his lap for his children to see. They knew to never talk during meals, lest they get a sharp strike across the hands.

My grandfather Sebastiano witnessed few moments of love and affection between his own parents, and so he avoided them with his own wife and children. No one ever taught him how to show and share his love, or even that such a thing was permissible. He came to believe that it wasn't. "*Il solo tempo lei dovrebbe baciare i suoi bambini in quando dormono,*" he would say.

This means, "The only time you should kiss your children is when they are asleep."

The children all had complicated relationships with their father, and one of them—Marie, my mother—realized at a very young age that she needed to flee his brutal control. And so, when she was just nineteen, she fell for and married a man she believed could take her away from her old family and into a new and happy one of her own.

But sometimes we are not drawn to that which is different from what we know and fear.

Sometimes we are drawn to that which is exactly the same.

My father, Nunziato Carino, was nineteen years old when he lost his own father, Francesco, to a brain tumor. Francesco was from Calabria, the southern region right in the toe of the Italian boot, and he was, like so many immigrants, a fiercely hard worker. He was a laborer for a snow removal crew in Long Island, where his family had settled. One particularly snowy day, he fell off a truck and fractured his skull. Seven years later he started getting headaches, and doctors discovered an inoperable tumor. I know very little about my grandfather Francesco because my father almost never spoke of him.

What I do know is that he taught his eldest boy, Nunziato, the value of hard work. Nunziato's first job was at age twelve: shining shoes. He never stopped working from that day forward. After his father died, he went into the army and became an aerial gunner, flying fifty-five missions. While in the service he faithfully sent fifty dollars each month to his mother. He was twenty-seven when he met my mother at a party; she was just eighteen, and shy and quiet and exceedingly lovely, and he walked right up and told her so. She demurred at first, but he persisted and soon swept her away. My grandmother Rosa, now called Rose, used the skills she had learned at Maria Cristina di Savoia to sew a wedding dress for Marie: a brocade satin creation with long sleeves, a fifteen-foot train, a mandarin neckline, and tiny buttons all down the front. Marie and Nunziato wed in St. Hugh's Roman Catholic Church in Huntington Station, Long Island; they had what was known as a football wedding, named for the thick Italian hero sandwiches wrapped in cellophane for the reception. They were a young, beautiful couple, sprung from the immigrant experience and poised to start a new American adventure of their own.

Their first daughter, Annette, was smart and thoughtful and mature beyond her years. She was rational, reserved, a straight-A student. Their second daughter was different: a rebel, a jokester, carefree, and questioning, so stubborn and argumentative her parents dubbed her "chatterbox." She had to have the last word, to the point where her mother and sisters would beg, "Please stop talking." She demanded answers, and she never left well enough alone.

That daughter was me.

Our childhood in Huntington Station was not one of material deprivation. We had plenty of food, comfortable beds, clean clothes, and toys we loved. In our first home, a brick ranch house my father built, Annette and I shared a corner bedroom with a double bed, rosebud wallpaper, crocheted comforters, and curtains with floral trim. Down the hall Frank had his own room, while Nancy, still a baby, slept in a crib in my parents' bedroom. We went to good schools, had good friends, and enjoyed a good measure of stability and routine.

And, like most families, we had pets, though the history of our animals is ramshackle at best. My father loved little creatures, starting with the Chihuahua he brought home from the war that he took with him everywhere. However, our family pets seemed to come and go at an alarming rate. One of our earliest cats, Casey, got leukemia and died young. A Yorkie terrier we named Michael got away and was hit by a car. We had a one-eyed black Persian cat that seemed happy enough to be with us, but when we got new furniture, the cat's shedding became a problem and he was given away. We also had a cute little golden Pomeranian who went missing during a snowstorm; when the snow finally melted a few days later, we found the poor thing frozen to death by the back door of our house.

I never expected the pets we loved would be around for long. It was just another thing I couldn't control. Looking back, it's not surprising the pets were never safe in our house. The truth is, none of us were.

My father liked to drink, and drinking changed who he was. I don't know precisely what happened when alcohol passed through his stomach, into his bloodstream, and finally hit his brain. I know alcohol dulls your senses and your mental sharpness. I know it affects alertness and coordination. And I know in some people it causes anger and agitation. But what happened to my father was something different. Alcohol utterly transformed him.

When my father was sober, he was one of the loveliest men you'd ever meet. Funny, generous, warm with loved ones, welcoming to strangers. To this day people come up and tell me how wonderful he was. People I grew up with say, "I wish my father had been more like yours."

But every day after his shift as a bartender at the Picture Lounge, it's as if he'd swap clothes with some other man and send him home in his place. My father liked scotch whisky—Dewar's on the rocks—and he would drink during his shift and stay afterward and drink some more. When he got into the car to drive home, what we called the dark cloud would come over him. His eyes got squinty, and his face grew tight, and his normal, natural smile disappeared into a hard frown. The demons inside him would stew and percolate and rise to the surface, awaiting the slightest trigger to explode. The trigger could be anything, even nothing. We never knew what it was that made him so angry on those car rides home or what would set him off when he walked in. All we knew was that once my father's rages had started, they could not be stopped.

Most nights we'd be in bed when he arrived at midnight or later. We'd listen for the telltale sounds—the way he slammed the front door or the clinking of ice in a glass in the kitchen, letting us know he wasn't done drinking. But sometimes there was no noise at all.

Sometimes it would just start.

My brother Frank would be sound asleep, and my father would appear in his bedroom, a dark figure in the doorway. And then he would scream and curse at the boy, as if Frank were a man he held some mortal grievance against.

"Frank, you miserable, no-good son of a bitch!!"

Frank, not yet six, would jolt awake, then lay there still, cowering under the covers. Five minutes of yelling. Ten minutes. It seemed

77

like it would never end. In the other room Annette and I would hear it and hold each other for comfort; down the hall we could hear baby Nancy crying in her crib. My mother would not always rush in to stop him; she knew defending Frank would likely make the situation worse and earn both her and Frank even more abuse. But some nights the rages were so scary, it was impossible for her not to go and protect her boy. Usually, my father wouldn't stop until he'd exhausted himself, and then he'd slam the door and go drink some more and finally, in the dead of night, pass out.

There was never a real reason for him to turn on my brother. Sometimes all it took was seeing something that made him think of Frankie.

We were all subject to those rages, but most of the time they were aimed at my mother and at Frankie. At dinner one night, Frankie simply asked my father to pass him a bowl of spaghetti. My father, drunk, grabbed it and threw it at him. Frankie just sat there, covered in sauce. Another night my father picked up a package of ten Flying Saucer ice cream sandwiches from Carvel on his way home from work. He set them on the kitchen table, and I was so excited that for a moment I forgot our most important rule: don't say anything that might provoke Dad.

I announced, "I'm so excited I could eat all of them by myself."

I was seven years old; it's something kids say.

My father said, "Good, now you're gonna eat every one."

The other children hurried away at this first sign of trouble, and my father sat down at the table and told me to start eating. My mother was at work and was not there to stop him. I got through one Flying Saucer, then two, then a third. Halfway through the fourth I started sobbing. In the middle of the sixth or seventh, I threw up. Satisfied, my father got up and walked away. The other sandwiches melted in the sink: no one dared come for them after my punishment was over.

We lived in absolute terror of pushing a trigger. When my father was at work we'd frantically clean the house and try to leave nothing out of place. Inevitably, we'd miss something, and that was all it took. When my father was home, we never spoke loudly, if we spoke at all. In our bedroom, when Annette and I quarreled about something, we'd argue in whispers. If I got mad, I'd raise my voice, and Annette would beg me to be quiet. I'd speak louder until, out of terror, she conceded the point and pulled the covers over her head. I won quite a few arguments that way.

Watching my father go after someone else was always worse than when he targeted me. One Christmas, my mother bought him a handsome beige suede jacket. My father, sober, loved it and slipped it on, modeling it, to my mother's delight. But the next day, drunk, he stuck the jacket in my mother's face.

"What am I, a pimp?"

Then he took those shearing scissors and cut the jacket into shreds.

Worst of all was when he hit my mother. I couldn't bear to see him do it; I'd feel sick and panicked and utterly helpless. I was terrified that one day he'd go too far.

There is one instance ingrained in my memory that has left an indelible mark.

Annette and I were half asleep in bed when we heard the yelling begin. I don't know what it was about—I seldom did—but it went on for a long time, subsiding then rising again. I didn't hear my mother's voice, only my father's. These weren't arguments. They were blitzes.

Then I heard a horrific crash—the sound of glass shattering. I was sure my father had thrown my mother through the big front window. Annette begged me to go and break up the fight. I was usually as scared as she was, but this time I was so worried for my mother that I ran into the living room screaming, "Mom! Mom!" When I got there, the window was intact; my father had thrown a brass lamp with a large glass shade across the room, shattering it. He'd also hurled a bowl of tomato sauce against a wall, and the green velvet sofa was covered in red. Chairs were overturned, and my mother was on the floor, bruised and bleeding. I ran to her, and to this day I remember the look of horror on her face—not horror at having been hit but horror at having me see her this way.

Later that night, after my father passed out, Annette and I comforted her; poor little Frankie was too terrified to come out of his room. In the morning my mother told us the same thing she always told us: "Be normal; act like nothing happened." The next day we went to school and my mother cleaned up the mess, and the incident was never mentioned, as if it had merely been a bad dream.

9

THE BROWN PAPER BAG

After my fourth consecutive Monday with Maurice, I told my boss, Valerie, that I had brought him up to my apartment and cooked him dinner. She looked surprised, then alarmed.

"Laura, I don't understand why you're doing this," she said. "You don't really know this kid, you don't know his family, you don't know if they will be upset with you."

I'd told her about meeting Maurice's mother, about how no one in his family cared what he did or who he did it with, but she wasn't convinced.

"Laura, you can't have this boy up to your apartment," she said. "That's just *crazy*." Valerie was raising her voice now, trying to get through to me. "You could have someone from social services knocking on your door and asking you what's going on. You need to be careful here. I mean, you're white; he's black. You're an adult; he's a kid. Something could go wrong. Things could get ugly."

I knew Valerie was speaking from the heart. She was my dear friend, and she cared about me. And I knew, on some level, that what she was saying was true. I *was* in over my head. I had no business inviting this child up to my apartment. What I was doing could very easily be misinterpreted. Though Valerie didn't say it, I knew she was also concerned about my safety. Her forceful words to me were exactly what I would expect a true friend to say. In fact, several close friends and even my sisters had told me the same thing. But in the end I had to trust my gut. I knew deep down—too deep for rational explanation—that what I was doing was the right thing to do.

"Look, Valerie, Maurice is a good kid," I said. "He's a really good kid with a terrible life. He just needs someone he can turn to for help."

Valerie wasn't persuaded, at least not that day, but over time, as I kept her abreast of my outings with Maurice, she stopped sounding concerned. She would later tell me she came to realize Maurice and I had a real relationship and that he was getting the kind of support that would have an impact on him for the rest of his life. "And who," she said, "can argue with that?" Isn't that worth a little risk?

My other friends and colleagues at *USA Today*—Lou, Paul, and the rest, all kind, good-hearted people—slowly came around as well. They, too, had been worried for me, but the more they heard about my time with Maurice, the less concerned they became—and the more they wanted to know what was going on in his life. They came to enjoy hearing about our trips and outings, and they began to ask me about him all the time. Lou, a sweetheart of a guy, listened to all my stories about Maurice and told me many times that he admired what I was doing. He had two small boys at the time and he said he could not imagine what Maurice was going through. Then one day he walked into my office with a big shopping bag.

The bag was full of clothes.

Lou told me he'd gone through his closets at home and gathered up some shirts, sweaters, and pants he no longer wore. He knew they were probably a little bit big for Maurice, but at least they were in pretty good condition.

"You said Maurice doesn't have many clothes," Lou said. "I thought maybe he could use some of these."

I looked through the bag. Stacks of shirts, pants, sweaters, shorts—everything neatly folded, looking almost new. A couple of items even had store tags still attached.

My eyes teared up. I gave Lou a hug and thanked him for the clothes, then closed the door to my office and had a little cry.

Maurice and I were settling into a nice routine. We no longer had to confirm our next Monday meeting; it was automatic. He'd just show up in the lobby, and the concierge at the front desk would ring me and send him up.

Early on, Maurice told me that the concierge sometimes made him wait before sending him up, either to deal with other tenants or make a phone call or whatever. He would shoo Maurice off to the side and only get back to him once the lobby was clear. Maurice said they treated him differently when he was with me versus when they saw him alone. He was used to this; most grown-ups acted as if he was invisible. Once, when he was running late to see me, he asked a passerby for the time. The person said nothing and kept walking; he didn't even look at Maurice. He asked another person; same thing. They not only weren't giving Maurice the time; they were pretending he wasn't there.

I understood why the concierge might brush him off. The Symphony was a luxury building, and here was this homeless kid in grubby sweats getting funny looks from the upscale tenants. I understood they were in no position to chum around with Maurice. Still, I didn't like that he was made to wait or that he was treated differently when I wasn't around. One night I walked out with Maurice and stopped at the front desk. I had Maurice wait outside while I talked to the concierge.

"I just want to say again that Maurice is my friend, and I want you guys to treat him like you would any of my friends," I told him. "This is my home, and he should always feel welcome here, okay?"

The concierge looked a little wounded, but he got the message.

"Of course, Miss Schroff," he said.

Before long, Maurice became buddies with just about everyone on the staff.

Try as he might, Maurice could not stay clean. His clothes were inevitably grimy and he usually smelled pretty bad, so laundry became part of our weekly deal. Then, one Monday, he walked in with a shopping bag full of clothes.

"Miss Laura," he said, "would you mind if, when you do my laundry, you could wash these for my family?"

I could tell the clothes belonged to his sisters and maybe his mother and cousins. I washed and dried them, and when I gave them back to Maurice, he was thrilled by how fresh and clean they were. Maurice, I soon gathered, was the man of his house. He was taking on responsibilities and seeing to it that his family had clean clothes.

After a while, instead of asking Maurice what he wanted me to cook, I told him he should come shopping with me. So we'd go to the supermarket and pick out things he liked—steaks, hamburgers, chicken, and, of course, chocolate chip cookie dough. At my apartment, Maurice would set the table while I cooked. After the first time, he did it without being asked. He seemed to like doing it.

After dinner, he'd help me clear the table and get the dishes in the sink. I'd rinse them and hand them to Maurice, and he'd put them in my dishwasher. One evening, when I was on my way to take the garbage to the hallway trash room, Maurice looked at me and said, "Miss Laura, let me take that out for you. A nice lady like you should not have to dump the garbage."

We were establishing rituals now—setting the table, clearing the dishes, taking out the garbage—and usually we moved through them without even speaking. He loved having these chores to do, and he was very meticulous about them.

I realized the rituals themselves were as important to Maurice as the meals.

Rituals are what ground us in our lives, what give us a sense of safety and continuity. In my own family growing up, crazy as it was, we still had set routines—dinner at a certain hour, in bed at the same time every night, church on Sundays. In the same way, to Maurice, a simple thing like taking out the trash was comforting on so many levels. It was, to him, almost sacred.

Of course, there was the ritual he loved best: baking and eating cookies. I knew now that he always wanted to take some home to his sisters, so I made sure to bake extra cookies. But then, one night, I noticed he hadn't drunk all his milk.

"Do you think I could take this milk home, too?" he asked.

He wanted his sisters to have the full experience—not just the warm cookies, but the warm cookies and *milk*. From then on, we'd pick up a half gallon of milk instead of a quart, so he could take some home.

Maurice and I were becoming comfortable around each other, to the point where I sometimes forgot who he was and just thought of him as someone I hung out with. Sometimes we'd play a board game, like Monopoly, and laugh and tease each other. Sometimes I complained to him about something at work, like I would with any friend. But every once in a while something happened to remind me that Maurice came from extraordinary circumstances. One Monday, he showed up at my apartment with a pretty bad cold. He was sniffling and snorting and couldn't get his nose clear.

Finally, I said, "Maurice, will you go to the bathroom and blow your nose already?"

He looked at me and said, "Huh?"

"Blow your nose," I said. "Go in there and blow your nose."

He stared at me as if I was speaking another language. And then I figured it out—he didn't know how to blow his nose. No one had ever taught him how to do it. No one had ever put a tissue up to his nose and said, "Blow." He had never even heard the expression. I took some tissues and showed him how, and then for the first time in his life he properly blew his nose.

One Saturday afternoon not long after that, my intercom buzzer rang. "I have Maurice in the lobby," the concierge told me. We were still seeing each other every Monday, and when I had time during the week or on a weekend we'd sometimes get together, but we had no plans to see each other that day. I told the concierge to put him on the phone.

"I'm sorry to bother you," Maurice said, "but I'm really hungry. Can we get something to eat?"

I said of course and told him I'd be right down. I took him to McDonald's for his regular Big Mac, French fries, and thick chocolate shake.

"Maurice, when was the last time you had something to eat?" I asked.

"Thursday," he said—two days earlier.

It broke my heart. I guess after Monday nights I tried not to think about all the other nights of the week and if he was managing to feed himself. I knew he was enrolled in public school, for instance, but I didn't really know for sure how he was eating during the day. But now I couldn't avoid the harsh reality of his life—that much of the time he was hungry and had no real way to find food.

Over our burgers I came up with a plan.

"Look, Maurice, I don't want you out there hungry on the nights I don't see you, so this is what we can do. I can either give you some money for the week—and you'll have to be really careful how you spend it—or when you come over on Monday night we can go to the supermarket and I can buy all the things you like to eat and make you lunch for the week. I'll leave it with the doormen, and you can pick it up on the way to school.

Maurice looked at me and asked me a question.

"If you make me lunch," he said, "will you put it in a brown paper bag?"

I didn't really understand the question. "Do you want it in a brown paper bag?" I asked. "Or how would you prefer it?"

"Miss Laura," he said, "I don't want your money. I want my lunch in a brown paper bag."

"Okay, sure. But why do you want it in a bag?"

"Because when I see kids come to school with their lunch in a paper bag, that means someone cares about them. Miss Laura, can I please have my lunch in a paper bag?"

I looked away when Maurice said that, so he wouldn't see me tear up. *A simple brown paper bag*, I thought.

To me, it meant nothing. To him, it was everything.

I'd known Maurice for about two months when, after dinner one Monday, he said, "Miss Laura, can I ask you something?'

"Of course, Maurice."

"My school is having a parent-teacher night," he said, "and I was wondering if you could go."

Maurice and I had occasionally talked about his school. I'd once asked him how he was doing, and he'd said, "I'm not getting into as many fights since I met you." That was one of the first times I thought I might be making a difference in his life, so I was excited to meet his teachers and find out more about him. I also wanted his teachers to get to know me. All the warnings from Valerie and my family had made me want to have someone from Maurice's life in my corner. To have his teachers know me and trust me would be a positive thing.

But most of all, I wanted to see Maurice in a school setting. I needed to see him in a situation where he was a child and not the grown-up he was forced to act like. I was worried he no longer had any connection to the innocent side of himself—that the streets had stripped him of any chance to still be a silly, curious, regular kid.

The sad truth is that I only knew Maurice as a panhandler.

Maurice began panhandling when he was nine years old. He only did it for an hour or two a day until he raised enough money—four or five bucks—to buy a slice of pizza or a hamburger and maybe play some video games. Most people gave him nickels or dimes or quarters; once in a while he'd get a wrinkled dollar bill. At first his mother didn't know he was panhandling, but eventually she learned he was working the streets and that he was good at it. She started going with him to have him raise money for her drugs. Maurice didn't like doing it and ditched her. Darcella found other kids in the neighborhood—four- or five-year-olds with drug-addled mothers of their own—to take on the streets as props who begged for change.

Maurice went back to being a one-boy operation. Vulnerable as he was, he managed to escape any real harm on the streets, except for one time at a Pizza Hut in Times Square when a patron grew tired of seeing him begging outside the entrance. The man came out, walked up to Maurice, and punched him in the face.

Maurice staggered but did not fall. He looked at the man and said, "If you're gonna hit a kid, you should at least knock him out."

Before the man could hit him again, the code of the streets kicked in. Several street vendors—immigrants from Africa who sold knockoff Louis Vuitton bags and fake Rolex watches to tourists—were right up the block, and they ran from the corner and chased the man back into the Pizza Hut. Maurice knew the vendors—they lived in the Bryant, too, six of them to a room—and they weren't going to stand by and watch their little friend get hit. One of them pounded the window of the Pizza Hut so hard it shattered into pieces. A police car rolled up, and the vendors scattered. A cop grabbed Maurice and asked him who broke the window.

"Do you know those guys?" the cop demanded. "Give me their names."

Maurice said he had never seen them before in his life.

The next day he stole that box cutter from Duane Reade.

When he wasn't panhandling, Maurice was going to school. His mother was on public assistance, and to keep the checks coming, she had to keep Maurice in a classroom. He did not go every day, and he usually showed up late. But, as I would soon discover, school was very important to Maurice.

When I met him, he was enrolled in I.S. 131, in Manhattan's Chinatown district. He was a special education student, which meant he took classes with other students who had developmental and social issues. One of his first teachers there, Miss Kim House, knew him to be a bright but difficult boy. She noticed he usually came to school disheveled, wearing the same dirty sweats every day. His hygiene was terrible and he smelled bad, worse than any other student, and the other kids would tease him about it and make him mad. Maurice stood up to them; he was tough and wiry and could handle himself. He never hit the other children, but he got in lots of fights, lots of pushing and tackling and yelling. When he was focused, Maurice was a hard worker, and he was smart. Miss House believed he might be one of the special ones, but there were many other times when she feared he would not make it—feared that the anger inside him would overtake him and he would simply stop coming to school.

She never knew what was at the root of his anger; in fact, she knew very little about his life at home until the day Maurice's mother came in for a face-to-face meeting with school officials, a requirement of her public assistance program. During class, Miss House got a message to come down to the principal's office. There was a disturbance, and it involved Maurice's mother. When Miss House got there, she saw Darcella yelling at the principal. She was agitated, angry, out of control, screaming, waving her arms and jabbing her fingers, and not listening to anyone, not even for a moment. Someone called security.

Miss House took Darcella by the arm and said, "Come with me." She took her into the bathroom, brought her to the sink, and splashed cold water on her face. She told her, "Calm down, calm down, everything is fine." Darcella stopped yelling. Miss House didn't know why she was mad, and she didn't care. She could tell by her bloodshot eyes that she was strung out on something. She stayed with her in the bathroom for a few minutes, bringing her down. Finally, the agitation subsided. Now, Darcella just looked tired.

"Do you want to come upstairs and see your son?" Miss House asked.

Darcella thought about it, then said, "No."

Miss House told her to go home; she could come back another

time for the face-to-face. On the way out, Darcella turned to her and apologized.

"I'm sorry, I'm sorry, I'm sorry," she said.

"It's okay," said Miss House.

Now, at least, she had some inkling why Maurice was the way he was. All of the boys in her special ed class had their outbursts and bad moments, but Maurice would get angrier than any of them. In his darkest moods he would just shut down and drift to the back of the classroom, disappearing into himself. At least now there was some context for Maurice's behavior. After Darcella's disruptive visit, Maurice stopped coming to school. He missed four days in a row. Miss House asked the principal for permission to visit his home and find out where he was. She went to the Bryant Hotel and saw what I had seen. It was a more deplorable situation than she could have imagined. Then she saw Maurice come to the door, and when he saw her, his face—like hers—registered shock. She could not believe what she was seeing; he could not believe she had come to see it.

While she spoke to Maurice's grandmother, Maurice cowered behind a bedsheet strung across the room. Miss House knew he was embarrassed. She stood next to Grandma Rose and told her Maurice hadn't been to school in four days.

"Is he in trouble?" Rose asked. "He been suspended?"

"No, he's not in trouble," Miss House said. "He's just been absent."

"He's a good boy," Rose said. "A very good boy. And you're a good woman for lookin' out for him. Thank you so much. Thank you so much."

Before she left, Miss House said good-bye to Maurice.

She looked him in the eyes and said, "You need to come back to school."

And he did.

After that, Miss House paid a little extra attention to Maurice. She figured out what it was that set him off—chaos, disorder, disruptions. His life at home was shockingly unstable, and more than anything he needed a little peace and quiet. Her classroom had two carrels in the back for reading, and when things got hectic, she'd have him go back and sit in a carrel. He loved sitting there by himself; he got all his work done that way. Maurice soon figured out Miss House was in his corner, and to him her support was like a life preserver. One day after school, he followed Miss House as she got on a subway and went to a bank in midtown. She finally spotted him lingering in the back as she stood in line.

"What are you doing here, Maurice?"

"I got nothing to do," he said, "so I just came along with you."

She bought him a hot dog and told him he had to go home.

Her kindness helped, but Maurice's troubles did not just disappear. He was still always late in the mornings, and much of the time he seemed exhausted—too tired to focus. His grades were bad, and he didn't seem to care in the least about making them better. His clothes were still dirty, and he still smelled bad. And he still fought with the boys who made fun of him. The only thing that gave Miss House hope were tiny signs of progress—Maurice was getting a little better at speaking in front of the class, and he was fighting a little bit less.

She also found hope in something she'd hear Maurice say once in a while. Usually, he shared nothing about his personal life with other students, or with her. But every now and then he would tell her something, and he would say it with pride.

"I went to Miss Laura's house last night."

When Maurice asked me to come to his school, I asked, "What about your mother? Shouldn't she go with you?"

"Nah," he said. "She's not gonna go."

"Maurice, I'm happy to go with you, but you need to tell your mother about it and ask her if she can go. If she can't, I'll go."

My brief encounter with Darcella led me to think he was probably right: she wasn't interested in going. Even so, I didn't want him to bypass her altogether. She was his mother, and I knew that he loved her, in the unconditional way children love their parents. I never wanted to do or say anything that would get in the way of that. Growing up, I was never allowed to speak badly of my father, no matter how horrible his behavior. I would start to say something, and my mother would cut me off and sternly warn me never to say it again. "But *you* do!" I'd implore. "*You* say bad things."

"I am his wife and I can," she said. "He is your father; don't ever forget that."

Maurice agreed to ask his mother and to tell her I would go if she couldn't. We had our dinner, cleared the table, and baked our cookies. Afterward Maurice asked, "Miss Laura, when you come to my school, are you gonna wear your same work clothes?"

I'd been meeting him right after work, so he was used to seeing me in my stylish dresses and skirts and sweaters.

"I guess I could come home and change first," I said.

"No," he said. "I want you to wear your work clothes. You always look so classy."

The Wednesday of the parent-teacher meeting, I met Maurice in my garage, and we drove down to I.S. 131. It was a couple of big, drab buildings on Hester Street; one of the wings was curved, sort of like a low-rent Guggenheim. I was surprised to see that I felt nervous. I wanted to make a good impression on Maurice's teachers. We walked into his classroom, where Miss House was waiting.

"Hi, I'm Laura Schroff. It's so nice to meet you,"

Miss House shook my hand and said, "It's very nice to meet you, too. I've heard so much about you from Maurice." Her greeting was warm, but I could tell she was holding back, sizing me up. She had to be curious about who I was and why I had taken this role in Maurice's life.

"Maurice, why don't you take a walk around," she said. "I'd like to speak to Miss Schroff privately."

Maurice looked panicked and froze in his tracks. He didn't want to go. Two months earlier, I wouldn't have been able to decipher his reaction, but now I knew exactly what he was thinking.

He was worried Miss House was going to tell me what a bad student he was and how many fights he got into and why it wasn't safe for me to spend time with him.

He was terrified he was going to lose what we had.

I looked at Maurice and put my hand on his shoulder. I didn't say anything; I just looked at him. Words were not going to convey what I needed him to know. I needed him to know I would never walk out on him.

I needed him to *believe* I wasn't going away.

I smiled, gave him a little wink, and nodded. His face relaxed and he smiled back at me.

He believed me.

Maurice went into the hallway, and Miss House and I sat in two undersized chairs.

"You should know that Maurice is very proud of you," she said. "He speaks about you often."

"I'm very, very proud of him," I said. "He's such a special boy."

"How in the world did you two meet?"

I told her our story, about our dinners on Monday, about my visit to the Bryant, and about how I felt Maurice had finally come to trust me.

"I hope I am making a difference in his life," I said.

"You are," Miss House told me. "Maurice is not an easy child to control. He's always late, if he decides to show up at all. And he's always getting into fights. He shows enormous anger at times, but he's smart and sweet, and lately he hasn't been fighting quite as much."

I could tell Miss House cared about Maurice. I could tell she *liked* him. She had a classroom full of kids whose lives were complicated, each with his or her own fears and insecurities, and she cared deeply for them all. But she could see that Maurice's circumstances were worse than most, and, instead of turning her back on him, she turned to face him head-on. She tried to make a difference. I'm sure she wasn't making very much money, but that didn't matter—she was still determined not to let this child fall through the cracks.

"Miss Schroff, I must say something to you," she said, leaning forward. "Children like Maurice are always disappointed in life. Every day someone else lets them down. I hope you realize you can't just come in and out of his life. If you are going to be there for him, you have to really be there for him."

Miss House looked me square in the eyes.

"You cannot just wake up one day and abandon this boy."

I had only known Maurice a couple of months at that point, but I already knew he would be in my life for a long, long time. I just knew that in my heart. And that's what I told Miss House.

"Maurice is my friend," I said. "And I would never walk out on a friend."

After our talk, I met Maurice in the hallway. He was nervous and wanted to know what Miss House had said about him. I told him we would talk about it over dinner. We drove to Junior's restaurant in Brooklyn; Maurice had heard they made the best cheesecake in the city and was dying to try it. After our meal, I told him what Miss House had said.

"She cares about you and she wants you to do well in school," I said. "She says you're very, very smart, and she is on your side."

Maurice beamed. He was clearly thrilled by the feedback.

"But here's what she needs you to do," I said. "You need to stop getting into fights, do your homework, and, most important, get to class on time.

"I know it's hard to concentrate at home with so much going on, but you have to somehow find a way to get your homework done. And you need to get to school on time. If your class starts at seven forty, you need to be there at seven forty, even seven thirty. You can't show up at eight or eight thirty. That's unacceptable, Maurice. Do you understand?"

I didn't let up on him. I told him how important punctuality was in the working world and how he simply had to get in on time, how it was up to him to take control of his situation as best he could. The more I drilled him, the more confused he looked until he looked away and started to cry.

I had never seen him cry before, and it broke my heart.

"Maurice, what's the matter? Are you okay?"

"Miss Laura, you just don't understand," he said. It occurred to me in that instant that Maurice felt he had disappointed me.

"My room doesn't even have a clock in it," he said. "I never know what time it is."

"Maurice, I'm sorry I was so hard on you. We can figure this out together. Would it help if I bought you an alarm clock?"

"Yeah, that would help," he said.

"Okay, then, I'll get you an alarm clock, and I'll also get you a watch. When you go home, hide them somewhere so no one can take them. Keep them next to you when you sleep. In return, you have to promise me you'll try your best to get to school on time, okay?"

"Okay, I promise I will," he said.

"I know it's not easy, Maurice. I know your life isn't easy."

Maurice looked relieved. This was heartening to him; it made him realize bad situations could sometimes be fixed. He could make changes to the life he was living, and, with a little bit of help, maybe live another kind of life altogether.

Maurice told me that for the longest time he believed he was illiterate. He'd been evaluated by school officials, and his mother had been at the evaluation. After it was over, she had told Maurice he couldn't read or write. He didn't think this was true—he *could* write, even though he wrote very slowly—but after a while he just heard it so often from his mother and his cousins that he came to believe it himself. The worse he did at school, the more it proved he'd never amount to much.

That's when I told him I'd been a terrible student myself, so terrible I flunked a few classes and never went to college.

Maurice was surprised by that. To him, I didn't seem like someone who'd had trouble at school. And if I had overcome it and become successful, maybe he could, too. Maybe he didn't have to be what everyone said he was.

10

THE BIG TABLE

I've always liked this popular quote by a well-known gardening writer, Elizabeth Lawrence: "There is a garden in every childhood, an enchanted place were colors are brighter, the air softer, and the morning more fragrant than ever again."

I like this because it captures the wonder of two things, nature and childhood. And because it reminds me of my happier moments in Huntington Station. It's not like we lived in the country—in fact, we weren't that far from one of the first fully enclosed shopping malls on Long Island—but we did have lots of trees and some woods nearby and backyards where we could roll around in fresh-cut grass. We never worried about locking our doors, and our parents never worried about us when we ran out to play. Huntington Station in the 1950s was a safe haven. There *was* something special about the time

I spent outdoors as a child—those days when my mother would pack up the towels and the Johnson & Johnson's Baby Oil and take us all to Robert Moses Beach for the day. Or when I'd chase a pretty butterfly in the yard, or think I'd found a four-leaf clover, or just simply lay in the grass and stared up at elephant-shaped clouds. Moments when I felt the world was a magical place indeed.

Maurice didn't have any place like that. He didn't have an enchanted garden. I thought of Lawrence's words when Maurice told me he had never been outside the city, not even for a day. He'd been locked inside the concrete mass of Manhattan and Brooklyn and Queens his whole life; all he knew were noise and traffic and congestion. The closest he came to experiencing nature was walking through Central Park.

Around our eighth week together, I called my sister Annette, who was married with three young children and living in Greenlawn, a lovely town an hour outside the city on Long Island's North Shore. I asked if it would be okay to bring out Maurice for a visit. Her children were around Maurice's age—Colette was eleven, Derek, nine, and Brooke, seven—and I thought he'd enjoy spending a day doing all the outdoor stuff they usually did: playing on the swings in their backyard, riding bikes, tossing a baseball around. Annette didn't hesitate.

"I can't wait to meet him," she said.

That Saturday, Maurice and I set out on the Long Island Expressway. He was wearing new pants I'd bought for him and a nice blue sweatshirt, and he was a bundle of excitement and nerves. He had no idea what to expect. This was the first time he was leaving the confines of New York City.

It would also be the first time he ever set foot in a private home.

On the drive out, Maurice sang along to the score from the movie *La Bamba*. On one of our Mondays, we'd gone to the movies and watched the film about the doomed 1950s singer Ritchie Valens. Maurice loved the movie and loved the song, and I had bought him the sound track. He played it all the time in my apartment and car. He'd belt out the lyrics and ask me to play it again and again. I got a little sick of it, but I was happy to oblige him. It felt good seeing him lose himself in a song.

We got to Greenlawn and pulled into the driveway of Annette's home. It was a two-story colonial on an acre of land with a sprawling, beautifully manicured front lawn and an even bigger backyard circled by a fence. Greenlawn was a big step up from Huntington Station, a solidly middle-class town. Maurice couldn't believe a single family owned all this property. The front lawn alone, with its gleaming green grass, seemed to him an impossibly luxurious expanse. Inside the house I introduced Maurice to my sister and her family—her husband, Bruce, a lovely guy who sold medical supplies, and their three beautiful kids. The children curiously eyed Maurice, as children will do with any newcomer. Their mother had told them about him—how he came from a poor family and didn't have the things they had and how they should make him feel at home. Derek didn't waste any time.

"Wanna see my room?" he asked, leading Maurice upstairs. The girls and I tagged along. I could tell Maurice was surprised to see each kid had their own bedroom. This, too, was a luxury he could hardly comprehend. Derek's had baseball pennants and posters on the walls; the girls' were frilly and filled with stuffed animals. He walked around wordlessly, taking it all in.

"Let's go play on the swings," Derek said, leading all the children out back. I watched Maurice play for a while; his camaraderie with Annette's son and daughters was effortless. To them, Maurice was not invisible, as he was to so many adults. To them, he was just another kid. I watched Maurice swing higher and higher, his feet lurching into the sky.

There was a lot about Annette's house that Maurice couldn't quite believe. A room just for watching TV? A washer and dryer just for them? A bathroom downstairs and two more upstairs? Most confusing of all was the dining room, devoted solely to sitting and talking and eating. Maurice lived in a single room with eight to twelve people. If he ate there at all, it was in whatever spot he was in when someone handed him food.

Young Derek, in charge of activities, suggested he and Maurice go bike riding. Bruce went to the garage and pulled out Derek's old bike for Maurice. They rode up and down the quiet streets and didn't come back for an hour.

Soon, it was time for dinner. Maurice sat across from me at the big dining room table as Annette brought out heaping plates of food—chicken, broccoli, mashed potatoes, the works. Maurice unfolded his napkin and put it on his lap, as I'd taught him, and he looked to me as if to say, "Like this?" I nodded discreetly. Maurice snuck looks at me when he held his fork, cut his chicken, and served himself extra mashed potatoes; I nodded and smiled, letting him know he was doing just fine. Annette and her family treated Maurice like the guest of honor, asking him questions without prying too much. Dinner stretched into a second hour. Later, Maurice told me he couldn't believe people sat around and just *talked* to one another over dinner. That was a completely new experience for him. I noticed he was the last one to finish his food; Derek and his sisters were long done while Maurice still had a half-full plate. It wasn't because he wasn't hungry or the food wasn't delicious.

Maurice was savoring the meal.

After dinner the kids watched TV in the den while my sister and I caught up on each other's lives. I peeked in a couple of times and saw Maurice curled up peacefully on the sofa.

"Laura, stop worrying. He's fine," Annette said. It's true, he was, but I felt anxious, like I was waiting for a shoe to drop. I guess it was ingrained in me to think a quiet afternoon at home could turn chaotic in an instant, but I knew that Annette had vowed long ago to create a childhood for her kids that was different from our own. Now, she had a family that could enjoy a fall Saturday without fighting or, worse, cowering in fear. It had taken her a while—years and years—before she could truly let down her guard and relax, even around her new family. That Saturday when Maurice and I spent the day with her family, I realized my sister was truly achieving her dream; she had the one thing that had eluded us all for so long: peace.

Finally, it was time to go, and the kids said good-bye to Maurice. I watched him shake hands with Derek in that way boys do, awkwardly, thin limbs jangling up and down. On the ride home Maurice was quiet; he didn't ask me to play *La Bamba*.

He'd had a great day, and now he had to cross back into his world. For him, that was the toughest thing of all.

I always felt terrible saying good-bye to Maurice, because I knew what he had to go back to. I wrestled with the idea that showing Maurice this other existence, where children frolicked and food arrived on giant plates, was, possibly, a cruel thing to do. What was the point of giving him access to a better life, then just snatching it away? Was it helping him or hurting? I thought about it a lot, and I finally decided that as long as Maurice and I talked about it and acknowledged the hardship of jumping back and forth between two such drastically different lifestyles, then it would be okay to keep doing it. At least he was seeing there were alternatives to his home life; at least he could feel carefree and happy for one day.

Besides, Maurice told me later, he was never going to give up what he and I had, not in a million years.

"So what did you like best about my sister's house?" I asked him on the car ride home.

"The big table," he said right away.

"The table? The dining room table?"

"Yeah," he said. "I liked that everyone just sat around and talked."

Then he said, "Miss Laura, some day when I grow up, I'm gonna have a big table like that for me and my family. I want to sit around and talk just like they do."

It was the first time I had heard him talk about his future. Then Maurice, tired from all the swinging and riding bikes, leaned his head against the window and fell asleep.

Now that Maurice had met my family, I felt good about asking him to spend Thanksgiving with us. Normally, we'd all gather at

Annette's house, but I had something different in mind this year. I had just moved into the Symphony, and I knew the building had an outdoor running track on the tenth floor. The track overlooked Broadway, which meant the Thanksgiving Day parade of floats would pass right by us on its way down to Macy's. I thought Maurice and the kids would get a real kick out of seeing the floats up close. Heck, I knew I'd get a kick out of it, too, so I invited everyone to spend Thanksgiving with me.

It wound up being a wonderful day. Annette and Bruce were there with the kids, and so were my younger sister, Nancy, and my brothers, Frank and Steve. We all hung out on the track while the turkey Nancy had helped me prepare roasted in the oven upstairs. And then, as we craned our necks to peer up Broadway, we saw them, the massive, magical, helium-filled floats. Slowly they worked their way down the avenue, swaying in the breeze, tugging hard at their strings. Seeing them from the ground is remarkable enough, but on the tenth floor the floats were at eye level. When they went by the Symphony, it felt like we could reach right out and touch them. One after another, these magnificent giants moved past us— big old Snoopy, Raggedy Ann, Popeye the Sailor, and a happily bobbing Kermit the Frog. Maurice and the kids were beside themselves, and, frankly, so was I; I hadn't expected the floats to be this close. It was like something out of a beautiful dream—these iconic cartoon characters drifting by, bright and colorful, seeming almost to wave at us in the wind. When, finally, Superman flew past, I was yelling and cheering as loudly as any of the children. Except, maybe, for Maurice. To this day I can still remember his face as the floats went by. The only word I can use to describe it is *awe*.

Besides my sisters and brothers, I had also invited our father, Nunzie. In 1986 Nunzie was in his late sixties and he'd mellowed quite a bit, but he still held a certain power over us all. When Annette got married, some of the joy of her wedding was tempered by her fear of my father drinking too much and exploding. She had shielded Bruce from Nunzie when they were dating, but at her wedding she could only hope for the best. Luckily, he was in a cheery mood that day, but we all still held our breaths whenever Nunzie was around. We were grown-ups with our own lives and we were no longer under his thumb, but the anxiety, the trepidation, was just something none of us could ever shake.

On that day, Nunzie was on his best behavior. I watched him zip up his windbreaker against the cold air. What hair he had left had gone gray, and his stocky body was a little stooped—a frail version of his former roaring self. I watched him talk to Maurice. I couldn't hear what they were saying, but I could tell my father was being kind to him, pointing things out and putting a hand on his shoulder. Seeing them with each other—seeing these two strands of my life come together—was both strange and moving. I couldn't help but think that the terror and uncertainty we faced as children because of my father was similar to the chaos that Maurice now had to endure. And if I couldn't go back and change what had happened to us, perhaps I could do something to help save Maurice.

When we were young, we slipped into roles that spared us from the worst of my father's madness. Annette was the perfect daughter, never doing anything to disappoint our parents. Nancy was the quiet one, overshadowed by her older sisters and happy to stay in the background. And then there was me, the rebel, the wisecracker—I think what protected me was my personality, which everyone said I got from my dad. Perhaps I was the most like him and that's why he didn't pick on me quite as much.

That left Frankie and my mother, and they became my father's primary targets. Frankie was the one who was most visibly affected by my father's rages, and from a very early age we all started worrying about him. We watched him get quieter and lose some of his exuberance. The more he was pummeled, physically and mentally, the more he seemed to withdraw into himself. As he got older he stood up to my father and yelled back at him, and they'd have terrible screaming matches—endless fights about nothing. But the constant pressure of my father's rages surely wore him down and, I think, slowly and tragically destroyed some part of him.

Still, there was nothing he could do, nothing any of us could do. Our only respite was the day or two after the rages, when my father would be extra nice to make up for his outburst. Those slender silver linings were, in fact, quite wonderful—they gave us glimpses of how great a father he could be when he was sober. We were drawn to him on those days, desperate to siphon as much love and affection as we could, but after another day or two, we'd start to brace ourselves for the next eruption. If he was nice for too long, that only made us more apprehensive. We knew that after one storm passed, another one was never far behind, and so we lived in a state of constant fear, constant tension. Only in our most hopeful moments would we dream of some potent, earth-shaking event that might fundamentally change him—some magic bolt of lightning to shock us all into a new kind of life.

We thought such a bolt may have struck when my father decided to switch careers from bartending to building. He had built the house we lived in, and it was reasonable for him to think he could make a go of construction. So he sold our house in Huntington Station for $22,000 and moved us into a much smaller ranch house he bought for $16,000 in the nearby town of Commack. With the extra money, he started a construction company with his friend Richie. He didn't quite give up bartending—he was still working nights in a bar at the Commack Bowling Alley—but the rest of the time he was busy building homes. We all prayed he'd be successful and maybe stop drinking altogether, and then, miraculously, we could maybe be a normal family.

Unfortunately the building business was short-lived. He and Richie put up four or five houses and plenty of cash came in, but my father was a terrible businessman, and money slipped through his fingers like grease. He was talented and a relentlessly hard worker and, by all rights, should have achieved the kind of success he craved, but he was too restless to stick with any one thing for too long. In time, he always found a way to sabotage himself. I remember a big blowout he had with Richie; Dad came home drunk and dug out the blueprints for all of the homes they had built as well as for some future projects. He put them in a pile in the backyard and set them on fire, burning them to ashes. Richie was furious when he found out and disbanded their partnership. My father tried to keep the business going on his own, but after a while it went under—and with it, it seemed, any chance we had of a new, more peaceful life.

But then, miraculously, another lightning bolt seemed to strike. Five years after the birth of her last child, my mother was suddenly pregnant again. I was astonished and delighted, and I couldn't wait to have a new brother or sister. Beyond this excitement, I allowed myself to think that the prospect of having another child and the reality of having a pregnant wife might just deter my father from drinking too much and erupting into his destructive rages. Maybe this would be the thing that tamped down his demons once and for all.

And, for a while, he did seem to be on better behavior—until a cold, snowy night in February when my mother was six months pregnant. Our family took the half-hour drive to Hicksville to spend a day with my mother's sister, Rose, her husband, Ray, and their four young children. After dinner my father and Ray announced they were going to a local bar to knock a couple back. They promised they'd return in just a short while. A pang of dread shot through me when I heard them say this. After an hour, I looked out the window and noticed the flurries that had started earlier had turned into a steady snow. The streets were solid white. I could tell my mother was getting nervous too, but none of us said a word about it.

Then two hours had passed. It was dark out, and the snow was still coming down. I looked out the window and searched desperately for his headlights, but all I saw was white. My aunt, sensing our anxiety, suggested we spend the night, but we all knew my father would never, ever go for that. Nor, if he had been drinking, would he allow my mother to drive. The more he drank, the more contemptuous he became of her. Not in a million years would he ever trust her to drive.

Finally, my father and Ray barreled through the door. It was obvious they'd both had too much to drink, and it was clear to us, if not to my aunt and uncle, that my father's mood had turned pitch-black. I was in a state of near panic, and I could see my mother was, too. Not only was my father primed to explode at the slightest provocation, but now we had a blinding snowstorm to worry about as well. My aunt had a big pot of black coffee ready, and my father drank a cup. But when she suggested we stay the night, he brushed her off and told us to get our coats. My mother didn't even bother to ask if she could drive; she knew better than that.

We marched to the car like condemned prisoners, slowly and quietly. My mother sat in front, and Annette, Nancy, Frankie, and I squeezed in back. We huddled together and discreetly held hands. I prayed under my breath that nothing bad would happen. My father eased the car into the snowy street and onto a two-lane road. I was afraid to even breathe, for fear the sound would set him off.

We drove in absolute silence. The tension in the car was nearly unbearable. The snow was heavy, and we couldn't see out the front windshield more than a few feet. The only good news was that the blizzard was keeping most drivers off the road, so we saw very few cars. But then, suddenly, and for no reason I could figure, my father accelerated the car. We lurched forward, churning snow under the tires. We went from thirty miles per hour to about fifty. The car weaved from side to side as it glided over the dense snow. My mother looked at my father in horror and begged him to stop. Just when it seemed he might lose control of the car, he hit the brakes, and we swerved wildly, nearly spinning out before straightening and slowing to a crawl. We drove at normal speed for a mile or so before my father stepped on the gas again.

My father was toying with us.

The car swerved again, and my father hit the brakes. We almost spun out, but once again we straightened at the last minute. Once again, my mother begged my father to stop. In the back, all of us were crying—quietly. My father hit the gas again, recklessly challenging the snow, ignoring my mother's pleadings. I was sure we were going to crash at any moment. Then my mother, scared to death, screamed for my father to stop. We all joined in, imploring him to please, please slow down. He didn't even turn his head. Finally, my mother raised her voice as high as she could and *demanded* my father pull the car over.

"For God's sake, stop this car—STOP THE CAR!!"

My father sped up even more.

Just then, two big headlights appeared around a corner, coming right at us. A bus was rounding a bend in the road. I'm sure my father saw it coming, but for some reason he didn't slow down or turn out of the way. He just kept plowing forward. The bus driver blasted his horn and, at the last second, swerved away from us. The deafening sound of his horn mixed with our screams and cries as he barreled past; I don't think he missed us by more than a foot. It took this near collision to unnerve my father, and, finally, he slammed on the brakes and stopped our car. Decades later, when I think about how close we came to colliding with the bus—and about what would have happened to us if it had hit us—I shudder.

When we came to a halt, it was my mother who exploded. I don't think I've ever seen her angrier. She rarely stood up to my father—she knew if she did, it would only inflame him more. But here, on the road, in a blizzard, she had to take a stand. She was not going to let this drunken maniac kill her children.

She got out of the car and went around the front and yanked open the driver's-side door.

"Get out of the car!" she screamed at my father. "GET OUT!!"

My father didn't move.

"Nunzie, I am not letting you drive this car," she said. "Now for God's sake, get out and let me drive."

In the back, we pleaded with our father to please, please get out. Finally, he did. But instead of going around and getting into the passenger seat, he started walking away. My mother slipped behind the wheel and yelled for him to get in. He wouldn't hear it; he just kept walking. I knew that in his drunken state, he was too stubborn to let her drive him home. He would rather walk in a blizzard. We were at least twenty minutes away from our house by car. My father, drunk and wobbly, would never make it that far.

My mother had no choice. She started the car, and, with the children screaming for Dad to come back, she drove away from him. Her first responsibility was to get us home safely. When we were far enough away from my father, she stopped the car, giving us all a chance to calm down. She assured us our father would be fine, and she said that once she dropped us off she'd go back and get him. She said she'd also call Uncle Sammy, his brother, to go look for him. This made us feel better, and we finally stopped crying as my mother, slowly and steadily, drove us home through the heavy snow. Still, I couldn't help but worry about my father walking along the road. When we got home, my mother called Uncle Sammy, then set out to find my father. She told us to get in bed, but we were all too shaken to sleep. An hour passed, and finally I drifted off. I was awakened by the sound of my father coming into the house and slamming the door. I listened closely, expecting my mother to come in and check on us, but all I heard was my father shuffling around a bit and then silence. It was another half hour before my mother came home. She had been out for over an hour in the heavy snow searching for my father with no luck. It turned out he had flagged a car and paid the driver fifty dollars to take him home. Fortunately, when my mother came in, she found him sound asleep in their bed. Had he been awake, our nightmare would have continued.

My mother came into our bedroom, and Annette and I comforted her, as we always did. We hugged her tightly and told her everything would be okay, just as she had told us many, many times. But of course I knew better, and my mother, six months pregnant with my father's fifth child, knew better, too.

Once the floats had passed, we went inside and had our Thanksgiving turkey. Maurice loved squeezing around my small table with all of us, talking and laughing and eating. I noticed he ate slowly again, as if he didn't want the meal to end. Even my father seemed to be having a good time. He drank a little, but not much, and his features never contorted into the dark scowl we knew so well. At the end of the night he shook Maurice's hand and gave him a tender pat on the shoulder. It made me think about what a great father he sometimes was, and might have been, if only he had known how.

11

THE MISSED APPOINTMENT

When my mother got really big and round, she checked into Huntington Hospital to have the baby. We sat at home waiting for any news. Finally, late that night, our father called: we had a new baby brother, Steven Jude Carino. He was a hefty little guy, my father said: eight pounds, nine ounces, twenty-one inches long. My father sounded nearly as excited as I was, and I took that to be a hopeful sign. I allowed myself to think an eight-pound, nine-ounce baby could somehow change my father once and for all.

When my mother was strong enough, she went right back to work as a waitress at the Huntington Townhouse catering hall. We needed the money; my father's construction business was gone and he was already on to some other venture. So my mother would leave us to watch the baby on Saturdays and work twelve-hour shifts. Even with both of them working, money was usually tight. My father just wasn't good with finances; sometimes, on a whim, he'd show up with an extra car, some used Cadillac he bought so he could fix it up. I knew it killed my mother when he threw money away like that, but I also knew she could never confront him about it. All she could do was hand over her checks and hope for the best.

One morning, my mother was supposed to take some of us to the dentist. She'd worked the day before and was exhausted, so she overslept and we missed the appointment. My father could have cared less if we went to the dentist or not; he left all those details to my mother. But, because he was badly hungover from a night of drinking, he used the missed appointment as an excuse to go after her. And this time, he really went crazy.

He started by cursing my mother and screaming at her in front of all of us. "You stupid woman!" My mother came into the bedroom I shared with Annette and got into bed with us, and my father followed her in. He kept yelling and cursing, spit flying out of his mouth. "How could you be so stupid?!" My mother pulled us closer to her and waited for it to pass.

But it didn't. My father left the room and came back with two full liquor bottles. He threw them right over our heads, and they smashed against the wall. Liquor and glass rained down on us, and we pulled up the covers to shield ourselves. My father hurled the next bottle, and then went back for two more. They shattered just above our heads; the sound was sickening. My father kept screaming and ranting, worse than I'd ever heard him before. When he ran out of bottles, he went into the kitchen and overturned the table and smashed the chairs. Just then the phone rang, and my mother rushed to get it. I heard her screaming to the caller to get help. My father grabbed the phone from her and ripped the base right out of the wall. My mother ran back to us as my father kept kicking and throwing furniture, unstoppable, out of his mind.

When he finally tired himself out, there was a knock at the door. My father opened it and saw two police officers—it had been my aunt on the phone and she had called 9-1-1.

"We got a call about a disturbance," one of the officers said. If he had stepped into the house just a bit, he might have seen some of the damage my father caused. Instead, the cops stayed at the door, and my father—by then calm and composed—told them everything was fine. Remarkably, they took him at his word and left. This time, my father had gone too far. The kitchen was absolutely destroyed, like a twister had torn through it. My bed was covered in glass shards and soaked with scotch. My mother quietly rounded up all five children—Steven was just an infant then—and, without bothering to gather any clothes, piled us in the car and drove us to her mother's house in Huntington. My grandmother took us in, and we stayed there for the next three days. They were three of the best days we ever had. For once, we didn't have to worry about our father. He couldn't touch us here.

But then, on the third day, I heard my mother talking to my grandmother, and I saw her start to cry.

"Your place is with your husband," my grandmother told her. "You must go back to him."

I cried, too, and begged my grandmother to let us stay, but this wasn't something that was open to discussion. This was simply the way it was done in those days. Wives didn't leave their husbands, at least not in many Italian homes. They just endured. That was what my mother's mother did, and that was what my mother had to do now. So she put us all in the car and drove us home.

We crept in quietly, terrified to be there. I walked into the kitchen, unsure of what I would find. The mess had been somewhat cleaned up, and my father had dragged in the backyard picnic table to replace what he'd destroyed. The hole in the wall where he'd ripped out the phone was still there. Whatever my father hadn't cleaned up was left for my mother and Annette and I to deal with. And, as always, no one ever said another word about the fight. We all simply went on with our lives, pretending like nothing had happened.

That was the closest my mother ever came to leaving my father.

After that blowout, my father calmed down. Having baby Steven around surely helped. My father adored him; he really enjoyed how funny and cheerful and smart his new son was. From a very early age Steven showed exceptional intelligence, and because he was so much younger than the rest of us, he got to spend a lot of time alone with my mother. That helped him develop more quickly. My mother read to him and played games with him and encouraged his natural curiosity—by the time he was four, Steven had memorized the names and birthdays and even the *death* dates of every U.S. president. My father got a real kick out of hearing him recite them. I noticed my father did things with Steven he never did with Frank. He took him along to work, and he brought home the 45s of popular songs Steven loved to play—"Winchester Cathedral," "Barbara Ann," stuff like that. For the first time in a long time my father seemed happy to be home, and he didn't go out to bars as much. He still drank at home, but he'd get drunk much more slowly. And because he wasn't alone, he didn't get the chance to work himself into frenzies like he did when he went out. It was when he was in his car on the way home from a bar that he would sit and *stew*. At home he usually just drank until he passed out, and the next day by the couch we'd find his big glass ashtray overflowing with cigarette butts, piles of ashes everywhere, and maybe even a burn between the coffee table and sofa. That, we could live with.

Then, when my father quit the construction business, he got back in the bar business full-time—only now he bought his own bar, the Windmill on Jericho Turnpike. My mother went to work there as a waitress, and when Annette and I were in our early teens, we went to work there, too, shucking clams and serving hamburgers. We also left Commack and moved back to Huntington Station, to a two-story colonial home my father built himself. It was set back on a side road, some fifty yards behind another house, and had a long gravel driveway leading up to the front door. Inside, the layout was whimsical. You walked through the front door and into the den, inevitably the busiest and messiest room in the house. The living room, on the right, was hardly ever used and had very little furniture in it. You had to walk through the first-floor laundry room just to get to the bathroom. My father used shingle siding on the exterior, and because he had some left over he shingled a wall in the family room too. Still, there was a cozy little backyard and big elm trees, and I was happy to be back in Huntington and have the chance to make new friends. Besides, between the new house and the new bar, my parents were often too busy or too exhausted to fight.

Around that time my parents began renting a summer beach bungalow on Long Island's North Fork. These were our first real family vacations in a long while. We'd spend a week on a cliff high above Long Island Sound, and we had to walk down one hundred steps to get to the water. We all *loved* the week we'd spend there by the water. I'll always remember staying up late playing games and eating breakfast at a picnic table in our pajamas. Life was different out there: happier, more serene. I remember there weren't as many fights. The beach was a place where all of us could take a deep breath and, for a precious few days at least, relax.

And so, for the first few years of his life, my brother Steven had no idea what my father had been like. He only knew him to be a sweet, gentle, caring dad. It wasn't until Steven was five years old that he got his first taste of my father's dark side. My father had a big load of sand in the back of his pickup truck, and he let Steven and a little friend play in the sand with toy shovels. Without realizing it, Steven shoveled some sand into the truck's gas tank. When my father got in the truck and turned it on, warning lights went off. The engine was dead. My father pulled Steven away from the truck and kicked him hard in the rear. He bawled so loudly my mother rushed out and scooped him up. Not even Steven—this little boy he clearly loved—was immune to my father's wrath.

Still, we went on, trying to live as normally as we could. I went to junior high school, made new friends, started dating boys. From the outside looking in, my life seemed perfectly ordinary: I spent a lot of time with my friends, hung out at the Walt Whitman Mall, and went to Saturday night dances at Bethany Church. But as I got older, the stress of my family life started to show. I was doing worse and worse at school. My grades were terrible, and my teachers said I never paid attention. In fact, I was usually too exhausted to focus. For obvious reasons, I had a terrible time falling asleep. When I did fall asleep, it wouldn't be long before some nightmare shook me awake. Sleep, for me, was never a respite from the terror, only a continuation.

About the only time I could truly escape it was when I had sleepovers with my friends. My best friend was Sue, a funny, peppy girl who shared my sense of mischief. I *loved* sleeping over at Sue's house. Her mother was a secretary, and her father worked at IBM. To me they seemed like the perfect family. Sue's dad was home by six, dinner was at seven, and everyone was in bed by nine. The next morning Sue's mother, who always wore an apron over her skirt or dress, would have scrambled eggs and bacon and sausage waiting for us. Glasses filled with orange juice were lined up on the counter with a row of vitamins sitting next to them. There was always a glass of orange juice and a vitamin for me, too. We all sat around the table and talked and laughed, and everything was just so easy and carefree. I could feel the tension drain right out of my body. At night I'd sleep without worry, fear, or apprehension, and I always woke up rested. I know it sounds shallow, but what I loved the most about going over to Sue's house was seeing how her father dressed. He'd head out to work in a beautiful dark suit with a crisp white shirt and a narrow dark tie—he looked like something out of a TV commercial. I remember wishing my father was more like him. The truth is, I was embarrassed that my father was a bartender. I hated that he worked at night, and I hated that we all had to walk on eggshells when he came home drunk. I'm sure

Sue's family had its own problems, but to me they were everything we were not—happy, loving, and normal.

Sometimes, but not often, I'd invite Sue to sleep over at my house. This was always a gamble—I never knew if my father would explode when she was around. One night, Sue and I were fast asleep in my bedroom when I was awakened by the sound of my father's voice downstairs. I couldn't tell what he was saying, but it didn't matter. I knew what was coming. I shook Sue out of her sound sleep and told her to get dressed.

"What's wrong?" she asked groggily.

"Just get dressed. You have to go home."

I hustled Sue out of the house at two in the morning, and Annette and I drove her home. I never told her why I did it, or at least not until many years later. I didn't want any of my friends to see my father in one of his rages. I couldn't bear to have them know I lived this way.

Around that time, business at the Windmill started going south. I'm sure my father gave away thousands and thousands of dollars worth of free drinks. Slowly and steadily, the Windmill dragged him under. At home, money was tight; my parents worked longer hours with fewer rewards. The screw was tightening. We hadn't had a major blowout in a while, but we could all sense one was coming. It was only a matter of time.

I was at Sue's house one afternoon when the phone rang. She told me it was my sister Annette. I took the phone, and I could tell by Annette's voice that something was terribly wrong.

"Get home right now," she said. *"Right now."*

I jumped on my bike and furiously pedaled the few blocks home.

When I walked through the front door, the first thing I noticed was the fake plastic mimosa tree we usually kept in the foyer upended and lying in the middle of the den. I held my breath as I walked in the direction of the screaming. Usually my father's rages happened at night, so I could hide in my bedroom, shut off all the lights, and disappear in the darkness. But this was broad daylight, the middle of the afternoon. There was no place to hide. I heard my mother pleading with my father. Part of me wanted to run upstairs, where the other children were huddled, but I just couldn't do it. I was sixteen years old now. I couldn't pretend it wasn't happening anymore.

I walked into the kitchen. The table and chairs, relatively new replacements for the ones my father had destroyed, were in pieces again. My mother was lying on the floor, curled into a ball. My father was standing over her, ruthlessly kicking her.

Something in me snapped. I had tried to break up their screaming matches before and I had yelled at my father to stop bullying Frankie, but this was different. I ran up to him and told him to stop and started hitting him with my fists. With one arm, he swatted me away, and I flew across the room, crashing against a wall. He went right back to kicking my mother.

I shocked myself by getting right back up. I didn't know if I was hurt, and I didn't care. I was running on adrenaline. I went up to my father and clenched my hand into a fist. I put my fist in his face and held it there, inches from his nose, and I yelled at him louder than I ever had before. I heard my mother begging me to go away, to leave him alone. I knew she didn't want my father to hurt me, too. But I held my ground and shook my fist in his face and flew into my own terrible rage.

"Stop or I will call the police!" I screamed. "Stop right now or I will have you arrested!!"

I don't know if it was my rage, an echo of his own, that did it. I don't know if my father saw the lack of fear in my face. I don't know if it was my threat to call the cops—surely the first time any of us threatened him in that way. But, whatever it was, it worked. My father stopped kicking my mother and just shut down. The power went out of him. His shoulders slumped, and he stood there harmlessly, looking confused and defeated. Finally he shuffled away. I went to my mother. Soon Annette came down, and then Nancy and Frankie and even little Steven. We all sat in the wreckage of the kitchen with my mother, watching her cry. Later that day she drove herself to the hospital.

She had a dozen bruises and three broken ribs.

They bandaged her up and sent her back home with no questions asked.

Over time, my mother's bruises healed. She didn't leave my father after that, and she never would. But something changed for me that day. Something was different now that I had stood up to him. It was like I'd found a weapon I could use against him. It was as if, for the first time, I saw a way out.

In many ways, that was the day I grew up.

12

OUTSIDE LOOKING IN

Not long after our Thanksgiving together, I asked Maurice what he usually did for Christmas.

"Nothing," he said with a shrug.

"What do you mean? Don't you celebrate Christmas?"

"Nope."

I pressed him on this, and Maurice told me his family didn't usually do anything. He could remember a couple of times when his mother cooked something special around the holidays, but Maurice spent his last Christmas all by himself at the Salvation Army. He had the free meal they offered, and a staffer took him over to a bin filled with toys for poor children. Maurice had picked out a stuffed white teddy bear for himself.

That was the closest he'd ever come to getting a Christmas gift.

I asked him if he wanted to spend this Christmas with me and my family. He quickly said yes and smiled his biggest smile.

The Saturday before Christmas, Maurice and I went together to buy a Christmas tree. We picked out a nice one from a sidewalk vendor and lugged it home. I pulled out my decorations, which included little red apple ornaments, tinsel, and colored lights. Then I played an album of Christmas carols, and we drank hot chocolate while we trimmed the tree.

After we finished decorating the tree we had dinner and, of course, baked cookies. Then I handed Maurice a piece of paper and told him to write down what he wanted Santa Claus to bring him this year.

"There ain't no Santa Claus," he stated, laughing.

"Maybe not," I said, "but you still have to make a list for him."

Maurice scribbled something down. At the top of his list he wrote *remote-control racecar*.

Maurice asked if he could just sit and look at the tree for a while. I dimmed the lights in the apartment, and, with the Christmas carols still playing, we sat on the sofa and stared at the tree, saying nothing. We sat like that, with the glow of the tree lighting up our faces, for quite a long time. Then Maurice finally spoke.

"Thank you for making my Christmas so nice," he said. "Kids like me—we know everything that's going on out there. We see it on TV. But we're always on the outside looking in. We know about stuff like Christmas, but kids like me, we know we can never have it for ourselves, so we don't think about it."

I marveled again at how wise Maurice was, given his circumstances. He was still so young, but he had a definite outlook on life, a perspective shaped by his experience. He understood precisely where he fit in society. He may not have known how to blow his nose, but he understood the way of the world better than a lot of people twice his age.

A few days later, on Christmas Eve, Maurice came over to my apartment. My sister Nancy, who lived by herself about thirty blocks south of me, was there, too. She had gotten to know Maurice and really liked spending time with him. When Maurice came into my apartment, he saw ten or twelve wrapped presents under the tree, and his eyes grew wide. He must have known at least some of them were for him. We had a lovely dinner, and afterward we sat by the tree listening to Christmas carols again. I let Maurice open one of his presents. I knew there were a lot of basic things he needed— socks, T-shirts, underwear, gloves, a hat, a winter jacket, things like that. Over the months since I'd met him I'd been mindful not to buy him things he didn't really need; I didn't want to be the "rich lady" who bought him stuff. But Maurice had never really celebrated Christmas, and this was just too good an opportunity to spoil him a little. I did buy him a lot of clothes that Christmas, but there was one special gift I let him open on Christmas Eve.

Maurice carefully unwrapped the box. He let out a little squeal when he saw the remote-control racecar. He and Nancy assembled it while I got dinner ready, and Maurice asked if he could bring it to my sister Annette's house so he and Derek could play with it.

Incredibly, that was the first wrapped present he had ever received.

Maurice and Nancy came over again on Christmas morning,

and we all drove to Annette's house. When we got there, Maurice couldn't believe how big Annette's tree was—probably twice the size of mine. Beneath it lay a million dazzling gifts, or so it seemed. Annette loved to decorate the house for the holidays: wreaths, a manger, tinsel everywhere. Maurice walked around in wonder. Before long it was time for all of us to gather in the living room and open presents. Everyone had a present for Maurice, including my nieces and nephew. I'd helped Maurice pick out presents for them, too. The children were nearly lost in a flurry of wrapping paper, but I could see Maurice got T-shirts, underwear, a hat and gloves, a winter jacket, even a shirt by Tommy Hilfiger, which absolutely floored him. He got his own basketball, a pair of sneakers, and lots of other little gifts. He couldn't believe all of it was for him.

Then Maurice showed Derek his new remote-control car, and the two of them pounced on it, racing it up and down the hallways, in and out of the den. I don't think I've ever enjoyed seeing a child play with a toy more than I did that day. At the big dining room table Maurice liked so much, we all held hands and said grace. After dinner Annette handed out sheet music, and we all sang Christmas carols to Steven's accompaniment on an organ—the very organ Steven had once played for our mother. I don't know if it was because Maurice was there, but it was the nicest, warmest Christmas we'd had as a family in years.

When it got late, Nancy and I helped Maurice load up his presents, and we said good-bye to my family and drove back to Manhattan. Maurice asked if he could leave his racecar and his other toys at my apartment. He told me he wanted to have them to play with when he came over, but I knew he was afraid someone would steal them if he took them back to the Bryant. That night, the only presents he took with him were a new parka and some other clothes. He also took home a shopping bag I'd filled with hand-me-down clothes for his sisters and some extra food Annette had packed for them. Maurice had experienced Christmas in a way he never had before, and he wanted to bring his sisters a little piece of what he had seen.

When Maurice was gone, I looked over at my sofa where I'd left the amazing Christmas present Maurice had given me earlier that day. He'd walked in and sheepishly handed it to me, mumbling, "Merry Christmas, Miss Laura." Now, I went over to the sofa and held it in my hands as I looked at the tree Maurice and I had trimmed together.

He had given me the only thing he had to give.

It was the white stuffed teddy bear from the Salvation Army.

Sitting there, I thought about what this Christmas meant to Maurice and what it meant to me. He spent it with a family that wasn't his own—and that was sad—but he spent it with people who had come to care for him and even love him—and that was good. He didn't have to go to the Salvation Army by himself. Instead, he got to see what a happy, loving family looks like. That Christmas, as I imagined what my sister's family must have seemed like to Maurice, I couldn't help but think that my sister was living the dream she and I had shared from the time we were little girls. Many nights, we'd talked about what our own families would be like—what sort of homes we'd live in, what our husbands would do, what kind of classes our kids would take. For Annette and I, dreaming of families of our own and wanting them to be safe and loving was more than just a girlhood wish; it was a survival mechanism. It was the only way we could rectify what had gone wrong in our own childhood, the only way we could undo what had been done. It was not merely something we wanted; it was something we *needed*.

And so, that Christmas, I thought about how Annette had made this dream come true. And I thought about my own dream and my own desire to have a loving husband, beautiful children, and a big home in the suburbs. Here I was, thirty-six years old, still single, still alone. Why hadn't my dream come true? Why wasn't I a wife and a mother? The truth is, it wasn't because I hadn't tried.

Early on, Maurice had asked me if I had children, and I had said no. This was true. But there was something I didn't tell him, something I didn't tell most people in my life.

I didn't tell him that I had once been married.

I met Kevin on a platform of the Long Island Railroad when I was twenty and still living at home. I should tell you that Kevin is not his real name; I've changed it to protect the guilty. I was working for Icelandic Airlines, and I'd see Kevin on the platform while I waited for my train. He was strikingly handsome, with light brown hair, deep-set hazel eyes, and a kind of easy confidence about him that I found terribly attractive. We'd steal glances at each other, and after a while we'd even nod and say hi. Finally, one night when our trains were delayed, we sat together while we waited and began to talk.

Our chemistry was instant. I found out he lived with his family in a swanky Long Island town about a half hour from where I grew up. His father worked in the city and had his own company, and Kevin was working for him. Not long after our first conversation,

Kevin asked me out on a date, and we went to a restaurant in Manhattan. I had only one agenda: to watch how much he drank. Annette, Nancy, and I had all agreed we would never date a heavy drinker. Had Kevin downed his drink too quickly or showed any other sign he had a drinking problem, I probably would have walked out on the spot.

Instead, we had a wonderful first date, and we fell for each other pretty quickly. Kevin invited me out to his parents' home, and I was amazed by how warm and friendly they were. They seemed so calm, so centered, so perfectly normal. They were reasonably wealthy and upscale yet completely welcoming to me, and I couldn't help but feel drawn to them. I remember watching Kevin's father take the family dog out for a walk. We'd always had dogs in our family, and we'd let them run wild in the backyard. But here was Kevin's dad, walking his Weimaraner on a leash. To me, that leash said so very much—it *tethered* Kevin's father to his dog and, indeed, to his family. It demonstrated a level of connection, of protection, that was alien to me. I think I fell in love with Kevin's family—and maybe even with Kevin—right then and there.

We got married in a ceremony that, quite honestly, I can't remember much about. I do remember feeling elated that my dream of having a family of my own was finally coming true. Early on, Kevin announced he wanted to leave the family business and set out on his own. I was all for that, and I helped him get an interview for a job as a consultant. Consultants go around from company to company, analyzing corporate infrastructures and recommending changes. Kevin was really smart and took to the job right away. He made a nice salary, and between his and mine we had more than enough to rent a nice apartment in Forest Hills, Queens. The down-side was that Kevin would have to be away from home Monday through Friday. That was hardly an ideal situation for any couple, much less a newly married one, but I knew Kevin wanted this job, so I made the best of it. I figured this was the kind of sacrifice modern couples had to make. I told him I would do all the chores around the apartment—all the shopping and cooking and cleaning—so that when I picked him up on Friday nights we could spend every min-ute of the weekend having fun together.

About a year into the job, Kevin was assigned to a company in South Carolina. I was hoping he'd be assigned somewhere much closer, maybe even close enough to stay at home during the week. I wanted us to start trying to have a child pretty soon, but I knew we had to wait until Kevin was around more often. I told myself everything would work out fine. After all, I had every reason to be hopeful.

Then one Friday night when I picked up Kevin at the airport, I noticed he wouldn't look at me. No eye contact, no wave, nothing. I had a strong feeling something was wrong. Finally I said, "What's the matter? Why aren't you looking at me?"

"Why are you picking on me?" he replied.

After that, Kevin started to change. Our phone calls were shorter, more awkward. He was less and less interested in sex, then not at all. We went to the beach together one weekend, and I no-ticed Kevin's wedding band was missing. He told me he was twirling it on his finger down by the water and had lost it in the ocean. I was shocked to see him acting like it was no big deal.

We'd been married for a little over two years when we decided to go to Aruba on vacation. On our first evening at the restaurant, he brought a book to dinner. Again, I was stunned. Was he really more interested in reading a book than in talking to me?

"Are you kidding?" I said. "We haven't seen each other for a week, and you're going to sit there and read?"

He had no explanation for the book or for anything; he just seemed more and more distant. I knew something was wrong; I just didn't know what. He finally addressed the situation when he called me from South Carolina one night.

"I'm really confused," he said.

"About what?"

"I'm confused," he repeated. "I need time to think."

"Kevin, just come home. I can tell something is eating away at you, but whatever it is, just come home and we'll handle it together."

"I just need some time," he said again. "I'm going to stay here this weekend."

That was the first weekend Kevin didn't come home from South Carolina.

I couldn't believe he wasn't coming home, and, even worse, I had no clue why he wasn't. On Saturday I called his hotel room, and a receptionist told me he had checked out. This was long before cell phones, so I had no way to reach him. All I could do was sit and wait and wonder what was happening.

He finally called me on Sunday night.

"You're young and pretty, and you have a great personality," he told me, "but I am not in love with you and I want a divorce."

Kevin ended our marriage over the phone.

My reaction to his call was sheer hysteria. It was simply too much for me to comprehend. My dream had come true, and now it was ending like this? I couldn't believe there wasn't some way I could fix it. Kevin never gave me a number where he could be reached, and then he stopped calling me altogether. I would hear from his parents that he wanted me to send him his clothes, books, and golf clubs; nothing else from our life together was of any interest to him. I think I was in a state of near catatonia for about month, crying inconsolably, leaning on my mother for support, asking his parents over and over what had gone wrong. They didn't have an answer for me; they swore they were as mystified as I was.

Not once, not even for a moment, did I ever consider the possibility that Kevin was having an affair.

Finally, after three long days of not hearing from him, I packed up everything we owned and put it in storage. I moved back home with my family a few days later. All my friends told me to contact a divorce lawyer, and, reluctantly, I did. It was this lawyer, Richard Creditor, who listened to my story, looked me in the eye, and said, "Ms. Schroff, I know you've been through the mill and I hate to be the one to tell you this, but your husband has a girlfriend."

"Impossible," I said. "Kevin would never do that. He's not that kind of guy."

"I hate to burst your bubble, but your husband is seeing someone. I've handled divorces for lots of guys like him."

Honestly, I *still* couldn't believe it was true, so Mr. Creditor convinced me to hire a detective. I gave him the only piece of information I had—a post office box in South Carolina where Kevin picked up his mail. The detective staked it out and came back with photographic proof. Kevin had another woman in his life; I'd been replaced. Kevin's "I want a divorce" phone call had been horrible, but this news was absolutely devastating. It shocked me to my very core. It destroyed a piece of me that could never be recovered.

I sank to depths I never knew existed, languishing for weeks in a state of deep emotional turmoil. For me, having a family was not just a desire, it was the thing that was going to *save* me. It was my only answer to the unsolvable puzzle of my father's cruelty—my only chance to be happy in a way I had never experienced as a child. And now it had been taken away from me in an instant. I was twenty-three years old, and I felt like my life was over.

My mother sent me to our family priest, and the kind old man told me I could have my marriage annulled. He explained an annulment would essentially wipe our marriage off the books, allowing me to move on with my life and get married again in the Catholic Church in the future. But I saw it in a different way.

"You want me to make believe our marriage never happened?" I said. "You want me to *pretend* he didn't do what he did?"

I had spent a lifetime pretending my father's rages hadn't happened: pretending he hadn't torn apart the kitchen; pretending he hadn't punched my mother; pretending he hadn't terrorized my poor brother Frank. I just couldn't pretend any longer. I couldn't make this go away just by hiding beneath the covers.

"No, Father, I will not pretend this didn't happen. It did happen, and it happened to me."

I filed for divorce. Mr. Creditor, who'd taken a liking to me and an intense disliking to Kevin, promised me he'd soak him for everything he was worth. I didn't really care about the money, and we didn't have much anyway. Eventually I confronted Kevin about his

135

girlfriend over the phone. It was one of the worst conversations I've ever had in my life. I hung up the phone and mourned what I'd lost, and I kept mourning it in the days that followed, and in the months, and the years.

Looking back, I suppose I dove into the marriage too naively, too eagerly, more devoted to a dream than to a man. I am sure that I loved Kevin and loved him profoundly, but is love, by itself, ever enough? Was I just too hell-bent on escaping my father and my family and, because of this, blind to what I surely should have seen? I am not saying I wasn't wronged—clearly, I was. I now know Kevin is someone who jumps from one bad decision to another, and our marriage was, sadly, just one of those decisions. But I have to admit, if I am being honest, that the baggage I brought to our relationship played at least some part in causing it to end.

And yet, I was still only twenty-three, with many years ahead of me to try to capture my dream, and I might have been able to bounce right back from the debacle of my marriage, had it not been for another devastating event that happened at the same time.

My divorce shattered my faith in people and in love.

But the other event tore apart my heart.

13

BITTERSWEET MIRACLE

The very weekend Kevin called me to say, "I want a divorce," my mother's uterine cancer from two years earlier came back from remission. Her doctor wanted her in the hospital right away for more tests, but after talking to me and hearing about Kevin, my mother refused to go. Instead, she insisted I come home so she could comfort me. And that's just what I did.

My mother didn't tell me she was sick until a couple of weeks after I'd moved back home. She didn't seem any sicker or weaker to me, but I knew from what the doctors were saying that she was. We'd all been terrified her cancer was going to take her the first time around, and we had prayed as hard as we could that she would somehow pull through. Because she is a strong woman, used to enduring pain and hardship, she did—she survived. I believe my mother fought so hard because of her children. Annette and I had left the house by then, but Frank, Nancy, and Steven were still living there. My mother did not want to abandon them to be raised solely by my father. She fought like hell to make sure that didn't happen.

Now the cancer had come back, and we steeled ourselves for another long, hard fight. I decided to stay at home for a while so I could be there for my mother. That was a difficult decision for me—I wanted to do whatever I could for my mother, but I didn't want to be around my father. I had already left him behind and, in my mind, locked him out of my life. I had dealt with him more harshly and definitively than had any of my siblings, who went back and forth between wishing he would just disappear and forgiving him out of their love for him. But I did not vacillate this way—I loved my father, but I refused to tolerate him. I was just too angry at him for the way he had treated Frank and the way he was so casually cruel to my mother. I couldn't stand to be around that anymore.

And so, just a few months after moving back, I left again. I rented another apartment in Manhattan, on East 83rd Street. My mother was still very sick, and I remember there were people who couldn't understand how I could just leave like that. But I felt I had no choice.

Not long afterward, my mother got even sicker, and my father checked her into Memorial Sloan-Kettering Hospital in Manhattan, about fifteen blocks from my apartment. I later learned it was my father who did the research, selected the hospital—one of the very best in the country—took my mother there, and drove in to see her *every single day*. He would stay for only about an hour—he was too restless to sit still for much longer than that—but at least he came every day, never missing even one. He'd kiss my mother on the forehead, hold her hand, and watch television, and on weekends he would bring Nancy or Steven with him and let them have their time with Mom. Then he'd get too antsy to stay and say good-bye and take off. I realize now this was all he was capable of. The tragedy of my father's life is that he truly did love my mother, and when she got sick he was terrified of losing her. He did not stop drinking altogether, but he'd been scared into slowing down. He could never change who he was, but at least he was trying.

I went to see my mother at Sloan-Kettering every night after work. We spent a lot of time together just talking, and those nights with her were very special. We talked about what Kevin had done to me, what my father had done to her, and about how the women in our family had to be strong because of their difficult men. She told me she didn't understand why God would let me get hurt so badly. But, she added, God would never give me more of a burden than I could handle.

"So, Laurie, I know this has been very painful for you," she said, "but you need to know you have the strength to handle it; don't ever forget that."

I began to see in myself something of my mother's survivor spirit.

My mother was taking methodone for her pain, which was getting worse and worse. Her oncologist, Dr. Ochoa, showed Annette and me how to inject her. He came in with a syringe and had us practice on an orange. He made it look so easy, but I couldn't stand needles. Over time, though, I got used to it, and injecting my mother with methodone became part of our routine.

I could tell my mother wasn't improving, and that's when I began negotiating with her. "You have to get better," I'd say. "You cannot leave us with Dad. You married him, not us, and we can't deal with him without you. And besides, Dad really needs you. We all do."

The truth is I didn't have to plead with her this way. I knew she was fighting as hard as she could.

One night when her pain was especially bad, I left her room to talk to Dr. Ochoa.

"She is getting worse, and she's really scared. What can we do?"

Dr. Ochoa told me my mother's will was keeping her alive. What she needed, he said, was for someone to tell her it was okay to let go. I couldn't believe what he was saying. He wanted me to tell my mother it was okay to die? How could I possibly tell her that? What would I possibly say?

Dr. Ochoa put his hand on my shoulder and said, "You'll know what to say."

"But, Doctor, how will I know when it's time? How do I have that conversation?"

"When the time comes," he said, "you'll know."

A few days later, my mother's cancer spread so much that it started to break through the skin of her stomach. At first it was just a little dark blueish blister, then several more, and over weeks they began to cover her stomach and lower body. My mother gripped my hand one night and looked at me with sad, heavy eyes.

"Laurie, I'm not going to get better. My cancer is too advanced."

left: My mother, Marie, and my father, Nunzie, on their wedding day in February 1949 on Long Island. My grandmother Rose sewed my mom's silk dress in just three days. *right:* My first communion, in 1958. That's me in my special dress with (from left) my baby sister Nancy (sitting on my father's knee), my brother Frank, and my sister Annette.

The Carino kids in the mid-1960s: (from left) Frank, me, Annette, Nancy, and Steven.

Here I am in pigtails hanging out with my high school friends Darcy (center) and Sue. The Mustang belonged to Darcy's parents.

below: An old photo of Maurice's extended family. That's his mother, Darcella (holding Maurice's sister, center), and his grandmother Rose (far right).

above: My friend Barbara and me graduating from Walt Whitman High School in 1970.

right: Me in my West 56th Street studio apartment at the Symphony. It was only one room, but it was my sanctuary.

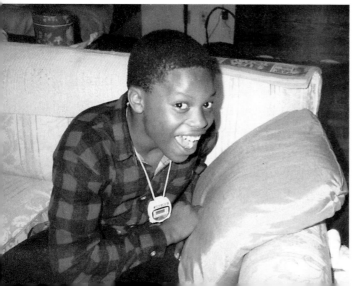

That's Maurice on one of his visits to my apartment in 1986. He's wearing the watch I bought to help him get to school on time.

left: I took Maurice to ride the carousel in Central Park in 1986. I could always tell he was having fun by his smile.

below: I took this photo of Maurice trying to fly a kite in Central Park. He had a little trouble at first but eventually got the hang of it.

above: Maurice and I on the outdoor running track on the tenth floor of my Manhattan apartment building in 1986.

right: Maurice in my apartment in 1986; he's wearing some sweats I gave him while we did his laundry.

Maurice loved visiting my sister
Annette's house in Greenlawn,
New York. He couldn't believe
how big the front lawn was.

That's my sister Annette and
her husband at home with
their wonderful kids (from left)
Derek, Brooke, and Colette.

Maurice fit right in with
my sister Annette's kids;
here they all are hanging
out in my apartment on
Thanksgiving Day, 1986.

We all watched the Macy's
Thanksgiving Day parade
from the outdoor running
track overlooking Broadway.
The floats seemed close
enough to touch!

Maurice opening my first Christmas present to him—a remote-control racecar—on Christmas Eve, 1986. My sister Nancy is giving him a hand.

The Carino kids, all grown up, at Annette's house on Christmas Day, 1986: (from left) Frank, Nancy, me, Annette, and Steven.

Maurice and my nephew Derek in 1989. I bought him a new Ross chrome ten-speed bike. Boy, was he surprised.

below: My future husband, Michael, and I at the Il San Pietro Hotel in Positano, Italy, in 1989. We'd been dating five months by then and got married eight months later.

above: My brother Frank in his navy uniform in 1975. He served for just under three years and got to see the world.

right: My girls! These are my poodles Lucy (on the left) and Coco in my condo in East Moriches, NY. Love those faces!

My sisters and brothers joined me at a memorial service for my aunt Margaret in 2010: (from left) Nancy, Annette, me, and Steven.

Maurice and his family at the funeral for his mother, Darcella, in 2000: (from left, back row) Maurice (holding Jahleel), Ikeem, and Michelle; (front row) Jalique, Princess, and Maurice Jr.

Maurice and Michelle helped me celebrate my fiftieth birthday at the Westchester Country Club in October 2001.

Maurice gave an emotional toast at my birthday celebration in 2001. "You saved my life," he told me. "The Lord sent me an angel. And my angel was Laurie."

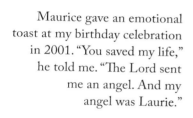

Maurice and his family today: (back row) Ikeem; (center row, from left) Jalique, me, Maurice Jr., Princess, Maurice, and Michelle; (front row) Jahleel, Jahmed, and Precious.

Maurice's dream came true! This is his family gathered around their really big dining room table in downtown Manhattan: (from left) Michelle, Princess, Precious, Jahmed, and Jahleel.

I squeezed her hand tight. I sensed her statement was really a question. Am I going to get better? Or am I going to die? My mother was terrified.

And then, as Dr. Ochoa had predicted, I knew just what to say.

"Mom, do you remember what you told me when I was so upset about Kevin? You told me God never gives us more than we can handle. You have to believe that now. God is going to take this away from you very soon, and then you will never be in pain again."

My mother gave me a sad smile, and we held hands and said nothing more. It was late, and I had work the next day, so I got up to leave. I leaned over to kiss her good night, and she looked up at me. "Thank you, Laurie," she said. "I love you very much."

We decided to bring my mother home and take care of her there. We filled the closet in our laundry room with big bags of methodone and needles, and I showed Nancy how to give my mother a shot. Even my dad practiced on the orange, but he was too impatient to learn how to do it properly. My mother had been injected so many times in the last year that it was getting harder and harder to find a space on her arms or legs that wasn't bruised. We just did the best we could and tried to keep her as comfortable as possible.

Once again, I decided to stay at home with my mother and commute into the city for work. At that time, my brother Frank was away in the navy, and we hadn't told him how sick our mother was. When we finally called him and arranged for him to come home, he was in shock to see how bad she was. I kept thinking of what Dr. Ochoa had told me—how I would know when my mother was ready to go. I wanted to be there when it happened—no, I *needed* to be there. So I stayed with her.

And then, on a Thursday night, around ten, my mother came out of a deep sleep and asked me to wake up young Steven.

"I want him to play the organ for me, like he used to," she said.

We sat next to my mother while Steven, in his striped pajamas, played some of the standards she loved to hear. "Please Release Me," "Spanish Eyes," some other Engelbert Humperdinck songs. He played for her for a solid hour. Finally, she said she was ready to sleep. I gave her a shot, she closed her eyes, and, in the reclining chair that had become her bed, she drifted off.

The next day, it was my birthday: I turned twenty-five. I felt like the end was near for my mother, but still I went to work. On the train ride in I kept hearing Dr. Ochoa say, "You'll know." I got to my office and settled in, but within ten minutes I knew I had to go home. I took the train home and found my mother in an unusually deep sleep. I'd seen her drift away many times, but this seemed much more serious. I could tell by looking at her that she wasn't just sleeping. My brother Steven, who was just thirteen, sensed what was going on, and he asked me if he could stay with my mother in the den where we had put her chair. I realized no one had really sat down with Steven and told him the terrible truth about our mother, so I took him outside, sat down with him on the curb, and had a talk.

"Steven, Mom is really sick, and she's going to go to heaven very soon. You need to get ready for that. We all do."

Steven just cried and cried. I put my arm around him and hugged him close. He told me he wanted to be near our mother and not in his bedroom upstairs, so I set up a bed for him in the living room right off the den. That night he tried to stay up as late as he could, but he finally conked out. My father wasn't working that night, but he couldn't bear to see my mother this way so he'd gone out drinking. Our house was eerily quiet. At one point my mother woke up and looked at me and reached for my hand.

"I feel strange," she said. "Please don't leave me. I don't want to be alone tonight." I promised her I would make sure she wasn't left alone for a single minute.

Nancy and I took turns watching her. Around 3:00 a.m., I went into Nancy's room, woke her up, and asked her to sit with Mom.

"Don't fall asleep," I told her. "You must stay up and watch her. I just need to close my eyes for a while."

Nancy, just seventeen, promised me she'd stay awake. My father had come home by then, drunk but in no mood to start trouble, and was passed out in his bed. I caught a catnap in Nancy's room, not far from the den. At five in the morning, I heard Nancy scream. I ran into the den where Nancy was standing over my mother, trying to get her to talk. My mother just lay there, breathing but unresponsive. She was in a coma.

We called for an ambulance. Just a few minutes before paramedics arrived, my mother woke up crying. I told her we were taking her to the hospital to get her oxygen. I didn't know what else to say to calm her down.

"I don't want to go," she said. "If I go I will never come home."

An EMT crew came in with a big stretcher and wheeled it right past Steven, who was fast asleep in his makeshift bed just a couple of feet away. Even with all the sirens and clanging and commotion,

Steve didn't budge. He just kept sleeping. I was glad he did; I don't think it was meant for him to see what was happening. I still believe God protected him from a frightening sight.

My father didn't wake up either. We decided not to get him up for fear he would just make things more chaotic.

Instead, we met up with Annette and went to Sloan-Kettering Hospital without him. Dr. Ochoa was there and asked us if we wanted a priest. We watched as my mother was given last rites in the emergency room. She struggled more and more to breathe and, finally, she stopped. Dr. Ochoa looked at her, then at us.

"She is gone," he said.

Annette and I hugged and cried. I felt my mother had hung on too long, had endured an enormous amount of suffering. I should have felt relieved that she was finally at peace, but all I felt was sadness, a deep, overwhelming sadness. I felt sad for what my mother's life had been like. I cried for all of the hardship, all of the affliction. And I cried for all the happiness she deserved but never got.

And then, all of a sudden, a nurse noticed something.

"Oh, my God," she said, "your mother is alive! Talk to her, talk to her!"

The nurse noticed my mother open her eyes. We looked down at her, and she turned to face us and gave us the warmest and most peaceful smile. We stood there in absolute shock. My mother tried to talk and at first her words were jumbled. But then, as if something clicked in her brain, she spoke clearly.

"I've been given the strength to tell you everything I always wanted to say to you but couldn't."

Dr. Ochoa was as baffled as we were. The nurse took my mother's vital signs and told us they were stronger than they had been in months. Suddenly my mother was perfectly lucid, and she moved her arms and legs like she hadn't in weeks. It was like she'd simply decided she wasn't sick anymore. But more than that, she seemed so calm and content; a strange, glowing peace had come over her. I stood next to her and kissed her and held her and cried.

Then my mother said, "Where's your father?" I told her he and Steven were on their way. Frank and Nancy were still at home.

"I want to talk to all of you," she said.

She was completely calm and in charge. I left her with Annette so they could have their talk. When Annette was done, she came toward me, crying, and said, "Mom wants to talk to you."

I sat down next to Mom, held her hand, and just listened.

"You have always been such a good daughter," my mother said. "There were times when I didn't understand you, but I know you are strong and good. Laurie, I am so proud of you. I love you very much."

I took it all in, tears running down my face. My mother never really spoke to me like this. She had told me she loved me and she may have told me she was proud of me, but to hear her say it now, in this way, meant the world to me.

My father and Steven had finally arrived by then. My mother then asked to speak with her husband.

"The younger children are going to really need you, so please be there for them. Look inside yourself and find the courage to be good to all of our children. Please try not to drink and fly off. Please, can you promise me this, Nunzie? Please?"

145

And then she told him she loved him.

Then it was Steven's turn. She told him he was a wonderful son, and she knew he was going to grow up to be a wonderful man. She told him not to be afraid, because she loved him dearly and always would. "I am so proud of you," she said. "You are so smart and you're such a special child."

Steven hugged her like he never wanted to let go.

Dr. Ochoa found us a private room, so we could all be together. When Frank and Nancy finally arrived, she sat them down for their talks. She told Frank how sorry she was for how my dad had treated him and how she hoped he would forgive her for not protecting him more. She told Nancy how sorry she was that she had to give up her teenage years to help take care of her and how grateful she was for that sacrifice and how very much she loved her.

Then she sat up and said she felt no pain at all, and her eyes seemed to glow as she told us what had happened when Dr. Ochoa had pronounced her dead.

"I saw the other side," she said. "It is far more beautiful and peaceful than we could ever imagine. I now know in my heart I will be able to take care of all of you from there. I will be able to look down and see how you are doing and make sure everything is well. Please believe me; it is all going to be okay. You are all going to be okay."

I found Dr. Ochoa and asked him if we could take our mother home. After all, I had promised her that. "We don't really understand what's going on," he said, "but if you want to take her home, you can." I told my mother we were all free to go, expecting her to be as excited as I was.

My mother said, "But I don't want to go home."

"What? Mom, what do you mean?"

"I don't want to go home. I want to stay here until it is time to go to my new home."

I was stunned. Everyone was stunned. We'd allowed ourselves to think my mother's instantaneous recovery was some kind of a miracle, that she was, all of a sudden, just *better*. But maybe that's not what was happening at all.

None of us knew what to do, so we decided to stay with her at the hospital. We were in her room when, about two hours later, she sat up, looked at us, and said, "Oh, my God, I have to go." Then she began speaking in Italian: "*Padre, vengo a casa pronto.*" We held each others' hands and prayed with her.

"Now, everyone, give me a big kiss and tell me you love me and leave me in peace."

After that, my mother lay her head down, closed her eyes, and slipped into a coma.

I stayed at the hospital more or less around the clock. Everyone came back the next day to see her, but this time she didn't wake up. My father and I were the only ones there when, at 5:00 a.m. on a Wednesday, a nurse came into the visitors' room where I was lying down and told me I should come with her. My father and I sat on either side of my mother, each of us holding her hand. We listened as her breathing slowed, until she wasn't breathing at all.

And then my mother passed away. She was only forty-seven years old.

At the time, I thought it had been cruel of God to bring her back and then just snatch her away. We'd all spent months and months bracing ourselves for the inevitable, and when it happened we thought we were ready. Then she rose from the dead, strong and healthy, and we believed she'd come back to be with us, to be among us again. But then, just like that, she was taken yet again.

Of course we soon realized God gave us all a breathtaking gift. He gave my mother the strength to tell us we would all be okay. He let us see she would finally be at peace.

Six months after her death, the night I sliced open my finger before my big interview, my mother came to me in a dream. I remember seeing her and running to hug her, and when I did she felt so real, so alive. I said, "Mom, did you hear? I cut my finger." And she said, "Laurie, of course I know." I told her about my interview and how I really wanted the job and how I was worried I wouldn't get it.

"Laurie, don't worry," she said. "You're going to do great in your interview, and you're going to get the job. Now try and get a good night's sleep."

Then she kissed me, and I woke up crying. The next morning I felt strangely calm and confident. Suddenly I wasn't worried at all—in fact, I *knew* I would get the job. I knew because that's what my mother told me would happen. And she was right. I got the job.

I feel like she's been with me ever since, looking over my shoulder. I've said I didn't know why I turned around on Broadway and came back to see Maurice, but that is not entirely true. I may not have consciously known what was happening, but now I have no doubt about what caused me to turn around.

I know it was my mother, looking down from high above, who steered me to Maurice.

14

A SIMPLE RECIPE

Most of the Mondays I spent with Maurice were quiet and un-eventful. Given my childhood and certainly his, quiet and uneventful were good things. On those Mondays I just tried to be a friend to Maurice and not necessarily a substitute parent. I didn't drill him with lessons in order to guide him toward a better life, but I did try to show him what was important to me in my life. I know that in that way, lessons were learned.

One Monday we decided to bake a cake from scratch: chocolate with chocolate frosting. I got out a couple of bowls, a whisk, a measuring cup, and a few other things we needed. Then I laid out the recipe on the counter. Maurice looked at it and asked me what it was.

"That's the recipe for the cake," I replied. "That tells us how to make it."

He didn't understand. He'd never seen anyone bake a cake or cook anything based on a recipe. He couldn't grasp why it was important.

"Why can't you just put all the stuff in there?" he asked.

"Because then you won't know what you'll end up with. If you want it to be good, you have to put the right stuff in."

I showed Maurice how the recipe worked. I asked him to fill the measuring cup with flour, and he did. I told him we needed precisely a teaspoon of vanilla extract. I went right down the recipe, explaining each ingredient, stressing how we needed to make our measurements exact. I knew as I was doing this that I was teaching Maurice something other than how to bake a cake. He was getting to see how discipline and diligence pay off. Perhaps he was even learning that what you get out of life depends precisely on what you put into it. Maurice whipped up the batter, and we put it in the oven. After it rose and cooled, we frosted it, and Maurice got to eat some of the frosting right out of the can. We admired our creation together for a moment. Then we poured a couple of glasses of milk and each cut ourselves a giant slice.

It was a pretty delicious way to learn a lesson.

Another time, Maurice found an ashtray in my apartment and asked me if I smoked. I told him I had, but that I'd quit. I told him why he should never smoke cigarettes or, for that matter, drink or do drugs. I told him what happened to your brain and your body when you doused it with toxic chemicals. I knew Maurice had seen with his own eyes how drugs could devastate a person; he knew that drugs were destroying his mother. But I still wanted him to hear me state categorically that he needed to avoid these harmful, potentially deadly vices if he wanted to live a happy life. I didn't preach these points; I'm not the preaching type. But I said them, clearly and forcefully, and it's possible I was the only adult who ever said this to him.

Once, he asked me when I was finally going to spend my quarters. He was fascinated with my giant jug of spare change, and it made no sense to him that all I did was put coins in and never take coins out. I explained I was saving that money for when I might need it. This, too, was a brand-new concept to him. He didn't understand what it meant to have savings. To him, money changed hands quickly and never lasted. The people in his life didn't have the luxury of setting money aside. I explained about my savings account and my plan to buy a nicer car someday, or maybe a house, or maybe just keep the money in the bank in case I had an emergency. I know it baffled Maurice to see all those dimes and quarters just sit there—thousands of them, good for at least a couple hundred meals. I imagine he may have even felt the temptation to take some quarters out of the jug. I can say with absolute certainty that he never did, not because I counted or measured them—he could have swiped fifty quarters off the top and I'd never have noticed—but because he knew it simply wasn't worth the risk. That old plastic jug of change taught Maurice what it meant to have savings, but it also taught him the valuable lesson of risk versus reward. It taught him to think *forward*.

Sometimes we talked about the future, both his and mine. I remember once telling him he needed to be "a straight arrow" and explaining what that meant: he needed to think about the right thing to do, pick the right course of action, then stay on that course

151

no matter what. We talked about how temptations can pull you off your course and derail your plans. We talked about what it takes to stay on course in the face of adversity: focus, courage, perseverance. Again, I didn't sit there with a chalkboard and a pointer. I just answered Maurice's questions and made observations.

From time to time, though, I *did* press Maurice about one thing: I kept asking him what he wanted to be when he grew up. I thought it was important for him to set goals and have a dream. I wanted him to not only pick a future but to visualize it as well. One night, Maurice was quiet for a long time after I asked him the question. I could tell he was really thinking about what he wanted to be.

Finally, he said, "I want to be a policeman."

Many years later, he told me why he wanted to be a cop. When he was young, he went to a phone booth and dropped in a quarter to make a call. The machine ate his quarter, the only money he had. He kicked the booth in frustration and kicked it again and again, and all of a sudden he felt a searing pain in his knee. He collapsed to the ground, looked up, and saw a policeman standing over him, holding a black flapjack in his hand. The cop had slugged Maurice on the knee, and now he and his partner were standing over him laughing.

"It took my quarter," Maurice explained.

The cops kept laughing. Maurice got up and started to run, but before he did he looked at the officers' badges.

"I got your badge numbers," he yelled back at them. "I'm gonna report you both."

He knew that even if he did report them, it would come to nothing. He knew there was only one thing he could do to stop cops from abusing the poor and defenseless. And that was to become a cop himself.

I told Maurice it was a great idea and that he had every opportunity in the world to make his dream come true, provided he remained "a straight arrow."

Some Mondays Maurice sat around and did his homework. After a while, he started showing up on Saturday afternoons, asking if he could just hang out with me. When I could, I'd stay around the apartment with him and play a board game or watch TV, but there were times when I had to run an errand or be somewhere. On those days, I let Maurice stay in my apartment alone. He told me he loved those days, because he could do anything he wanted—eat, read, watch a movie, take a nap—and nobody could bother him. Those were the first times in his life he had a real home—with food and water and electricity—all to himself.

Some Mondays we went shopping for clothes. I was careful not to buy Maurice too many things, and I never bought him any flashy, designer clothes, except for at Christmas. I just got him what he needed when he needed it. Most Mondays we went shopping for food, and we'd pick up the turkey and roast beef and other cold cuts I used to make the sandwiches I was now leaving for him with the doormen. I tried to make the sandwiches as hefty as I could, because I knew they might be his only meal of the day. I added fruit or applesauce or pickles and, always, fresh cookies, his favorite. I made sure to always put his lunch in a brown paper bag, just as he had asked. Sometimes, on Fridays, I'd leave a little envelope with ten dollars in it along with the sandwich. I wanted Maurice to be able to buy food over the weekend.

Then, one Saturday afternoon, Maurice had the concierge ring me from the lobby. When he came up, he was in tears. I'd seen Maurice cry only once, and I knew him to be an extremely tough little boy. I sat him down, brought him some juice, and asked him what was wrong.

"My mother got caught selling drugs, and now she's in jail," he said.

He'd spoken to me about his mother only one time, when he told me she stayed home to cook and clean. Now, he opened up to me about her.

"She's in Riker's Island," he said. "Riker's is a really bad place with really bad people."

We sat and talked about his mother for a long time. He told me she'd been arrested before, and he never knew when she would get out of jail and come home again. He had no idea how long she'd be in jail this time, either. He admitted he had lied to me about what his mother did; he had gotten the idea to say she was a stay-at-home mom from TV commercials. He admitted she was a drug addict and that she stole things to sell and pay for her habit. She cashed in all their food stamps and used the money for drugs, and that was why they seldom had anything to eat at home. Her addiction had gotten worse once she started using crack.

He said the reason he didn't tell me about her was because he thought it would scare me away.

"I hate that my mother is a crack addict," he said.

I didn't say much to Maurice; mostly, I just listened. I didn't want to pass judgment on her. I knew about parents with dangerous, destructive habits, and I knew there was no cheap wisdom I could hope to impart. I couldn't tell Maurice everything was going to be okay; I could be pretty sure that once his mother got out of prison, she'd go right back to using and dealing. I figured Maurice just needed someone to listen to him. And so I let him talk.

Later, he told me this was the first time in his life he felt he had someone he could turn to with a problem.

Maurice's mother was still in jail when his birthday rolled around in April. I resolved to give him the best birthday celebration he'd ever had. I asked him what he liked to do in his wildest dreams, and it didn't take him long to answer.

"Can we go out to Annette's?" he asked.

His wildest dream was hanging out in the suburbs with my sister and her family. I told him of course, but pushed him to think of something else.

He pondered it some more, then mentioned there was a wrestling event coming up at Madison Square Garden. It was called Wrestlemania, and all the best professional wrestlers would be there. He rattled off some names I'd never heard of: Hulk Hogan, Ricky Steamboat, Randy Savage, "Rowdy" Roddy Piper. He had talked about wrestling before, and I knew it was one of the very few things he seemed to genuinely enjoy.

"Laurie," he said—by then he had heard my nieces and nephew call me Aunt Laurie, and he asked if he could call me that—"could we go to Wrestlemania?"

"Let me look into it," I said.

I called the Garden and bought the best tickets available. I wrapped them in a box and handed them to Maurice a few days before his birthday. "An early gift," I told him. He jumped so high he nearly scraped the ceiling when he saw the tickets. We went to Wrestlemania together, and Maurice screamed at the top of his lungs for the next two hours. The Garden was packed with thousands of excited kids, all around Maurice's age. I was so happy that, for one night at least, he could be just another kid in this delirious crowd.

Part two of his birthday celebration was a Saturday night dinner at the Hard Rock Café. I invited my sister Nancy and my brother, Steve to come along. Maurice asked if he could have steak again, and this time he knew how to cut it with his knife. The waitress brought over a small cake with candles, and the whole restaurant sang "Happy Birthday" to him.

The next day, a Sunday, we drove out to Annette's house for a birthday dinner—part three. Maurice got another cake and more presents. On the way home, he was so tired he fell right asleep. I'd like to think visions of pile-diving wrestlers in crazy spandex suits were dancing in his head.

Back in the city I parked the car and walked Maurice home. He gave me a big kiss on the cheek and thanked me for his birthday.

"It was the best birthday I ever had," he said.

He turned to go, but then he stopped and faced me again.

"Bye, Laurie," he said. "I love you."

It was the first time he said that to me.

15

THE NEW BICYCLE

Maurice's mother was released from Riker's Island shortly after we had celebrated his birthday. She came out of prison clean and sober, healthier than she'd been in years. This was a pattern for many hardcore addicts: years of horrific drug abuse that turned them into zombies and pushed them to the brink of death, followed by a jail term that literally saved their lives. The time in prison allowed their bodies and brains to heal and bought them at least a few more years of life. But for many, this new energy and resilience only made it easier to jump back into the world of drugs, starting the cycle again. Maurice's mother stayed clean for a few weeks after returning to the Bryant, but, sadly, she was back on crack before long.

Maurice and I continued meeting every Monday and many Saturday afternoons for the next two years. At least once every few weeks we went out for Saturday dinners at my sister Annette's house, still one of Maurice's favorite things to do. I was continually amazed at how often Maurice would experience something for the first time. I remember one Christmas Eve at Annette's when her daughter Brooke came home from a friend's house crying. She'd mentioned Santa Claus to her friends, and they laughed at her for believing he was real. When she came home, she asked her brother and sister if this was true. They said yes, and Brooke was inconsolable. That evening we were all due at church for a Christmas pageant. Brooke, playing an angel, was decked out in her wings and halo, but she was still distraught about Santa Claus and couldn't stop crying. We had our coats on and were almost out the door, but Brooke refused to go. Maurice was watching this unfold. He could see Brooke's tantrum was making us late. He watched as Bruce approached his weeping daughter. He'd seen fathers handle situations like this before. He felt sure he knew what was coming.

Bruce sat next to Brooke and put his arms around her, stroking her hair. He told her everything would be okay and held her until she stopped crying. Maurice could not believe what he'd seen. In his world, a crying child would have been yelled at and probably hit.

He later told me this was the first time he ever saw a parent comfort a child who was sad.

For Maurice's fifteenth birthday, I decided I wanted to buy him his first bike. He loved riding with my nephew, and I'm sure he envied Derek's flashy bicycle. A few weeks before his birthday I drove out to Greenlawn, and Bruce, Annette, and Derek took me to the local bike shop. There, I spotted a Ross chrome ten-speeder that was just stunning. We all had the same thought: such a nice bike could be dangerous for Maurice to own. I knew he could never bring the bike to the Bryant; it would be stripped or stolen within minutes. But I didn't think Maurice should be prohibited from owning a nice bicycle simply because of his circumstances. It wasn't his fault he lived like he did; he was just a boy. I figured as long as he kept it in the bike room at the Symphony and watched where he took it, it would be okay for him to have it.

So I bought the Ross and had them hold it until we picked it up on Maurice's birthday. I told Maurice it was Derek who was getting a new bicycle, and we were going with him to get it. Everyone came along: Bruce and Annette and all three kids. Suddenly, the manager came around from the back of the store pushing a gleaming new bicycle with a big red bow on it. He wheeled it up to Maurice and said, "Congratulations on your new bike, kid."

Maurice pointed at Derek and said, "No, that's for him."

And then all at once we howled, "SURPRISE!"

It took Maurice a good two minutes to truly comprehend the bike was his.

We took it back to Annette's, and Maurice and Derek went riding for hours, until Bruce called them in for dinner. Even then Maurice didn't want to stop.

I think back to that day quite often. I think about Maurice's surprise and about his unbridled bliss as he peddled it madly that afternoon. I think about the innocence of that moment—the purity of his reaction. I think about what it must have meant to him to own something like the Ross. But I also think about how fleeting such moments of innocence are, about how good intentions and wide-eyed optimism and even love can only protect us from the harsh, corrupting reality of life for so long. Getting that shiny Ross bicycle was surely magical for Maurice.

But magic, like Santa Claus, isn't real.

Just a couple of weeks after buying Maurice his bike, I got a call from Nancy. She said she wanted to fix me up with a guy she had met through work. I was thirty-eight years old, and I'd been divorced for over a decade. I'd been out on a bunch of dates since then and had a couple of relationships that had at least gotten off the ground, but nothing had ever really clicked for me romantically. As I got older, I began to wonder if it ever would, but I still had the same dream—to have a family of my own—and I wasn't ready to give that up. I wasn't all that crazy about blind dates, but I told my sister to go ahead and set it up.

Michael and his uncle ran a lucrative business renting cars to travelers in Europe. He was divorced and had two sons, one graduating college and the other about to start. We joined my sister and her fiancé, John, at El Quijote, a traditional Mexican restaurant in the Chelsea district of Manhattan. I remember I wore a smart blue business suit and had lobster. I also remember I hadn't felt that comfortable on a date in a long, long time. Michael was warm and funny and gracious and sophisticated, and I said good night thinking that I liked him.

He called me up a couple of days later and asked for a second date, and we went to a restaurant in my neighborhood. We'd talked about Mandy Patinkin, and Michael showed up with a CD of his songs. On our third date Michael picked me up at my apartment and presented me with a pack of L&M cigarettes. He knew I no longer smoked, so I was confused. But then I got it: the L&M was for Laura and Michael. For our fourth date we went to a restaurant in the suburb of White Plains, where he lived. I followed him there in my car, and at a toll booth an attendant said, "That fine-looking gentleman ahead of you paid the twenty-five-cent toll for you." *Nice*, I thought. *Classy*. It's only a quarter, but still.

I told Maurice about Michael right after our first date. I said I had met this guy, and he was nice, and I was interested in seeing where it would go. Maurice would occasionally ask me why I didn't have a boyfriend, and I'd always shrug him off. Now I wanted to be upfront with him, because I thought he might worry a boyfriend would change our arrangement or maybe even end it. I wanted to assure him that would never happen. Maurice seemed genuinely excited and happy for me.

"It's about time you met someone nice," he said. "Someone who is gonna take care of *you*."

And, just as I had told Maurice about Michael, I told Michael about Maurice. I told him about this amazing kid I'd met on the street and how we'd become friends and how we met every single Monday and how we were important parts of each other's lives. Michael nodded and said, "That's great," but he didn't seem especially curious about it. I was used to people asking a lot of questions about Maurice, but Michael just didn't.

Over Memorial Day weekend we went up to see his brand-new boat, a thirty-six-foot Grand Banks trawler that had just arrived from Singapore. He named it *Paddington Station*. I hadn't spent much time on a boat, but I took to it right away. When Michael asked me to go on a two-week cruise with him starting the Fourth of July weekend, I immediately said yes.

Then I talked to Maurice about it. I'd have to miss two of our Mondays in a row, the first real interruption in our schedule since we'd met. Once again, Maurice was amazing: he told me he was excited for me and not to worry about him, and how I deserved to be treated nicely, and go have fun. He made me feel like it was okay to go, but still I felt a real tug in my gut about missing two of our Mondays. I remembered what Miss House had said: *you cannot just wake up one day and abandon this boy*. But I wasn't doing that; I was just taking two Mondays off. Even so, I couldn't shake the feeling I was somehow letting Maurice down.

After our boat trip, Michael asked me to move in with him in Westchester. By then, I was completely in love; I felt Michael offered me everything I could hope for in a man. He was kind, attentive, and generous, and he seemed like an amazing father. Plus, he didn't have a temper or drink too much. I was eager to move in with him, but I felt that same tug in my gut: *what about Maurice?* We lived only two blocks from each other in Manhattan, and Maurice could just drop by and hang out. Now I'd be leaving the city and moving to a suburb forty-five minutes away. When I thought about sitting Maurice down and telling him, it made me want to cry. It was like a riddle that had no answer: *how do I follow my heart and be with Michael but not give up what I have with Maurice?*

Oddly enough, Maurice was about to move, too. His mother had been awarded her own apartment in Brooklyn under Section 8, a federal program that subsidized housing for low-income families. This would be the very first real home Maurice had ever had.

He was set to move on Labor Day weekend—the very weekend I planned to move in with Michael. Seeing that Maurice was excited about his own move lessened some of my guilt, but not by much. I knew that even if Maurice moved to Brooklyn, he could easily come into Manhattan to see me, but once I moved to Westchester, our special arrangement would be changed forever.

When I sat him down and told him I was moving, I couldn't stop myself from crying. We were still going to meet every Monday in the city, and we'd still talk on the phone and otherwise keep up our friendship, yet I felt a deep sadness that something special between us—the sweetness of baking cookies in my apartment, of seeing Maurice set the table and do his laundry and trim the Christmas tree—was being lost. Once again, Maurice rescued me from my anguish.

"Laurie, we'll still see each other every Monday," he said. "We can still go to the Hard Rock. Everything is gonna be just the same."

This kid from the streets was reassuring *me* it was okay to go to Westchester.

Then Maurice said, "Don't worry about me. I'm gonna be just fine. Laurie, this is your time now."

I packed up everything I owned and had it moved to White Plains, and on Labor Day weekend I drove up to my new home, a fairly nondescript, split-level ranch house with a stream running through the backyard. I told Maurice to call me as soon as he was settled into his new apartment. He had packed up his belongings, too—everything except his bike, which would stay in the bike room at the Symphony. I'd tipped the doormen to let Maurice come get it whenever he wanted. Maurice didn't call me that weekend, and I got worried. Finally, that Monday, he called. He was crying so hard I couldn't understand what he was saying. I told him to calm down and tell me what had happened. Maurice caught his breath and spit it out.

"My bike got stolen," he said. "And my mom got arrested."

Maurice told me he'd been riding his bike around midtown Manhattan and made the mistake of keeping it out too late. I'd made him promise to never ride after dark, and he had stuck to that promise. But on the weekend of his move, for whatever reason, he was riding at night. He said two older boys jumped him and knocked him down and sped away on his shiny Ross. He said he tried to chase them, but couldn't catch up. He said he felt terrible that this bike I had given him was gone, and I told him it was okay.

"It's just a bike; as long as you're not hurt." But I knew that to Maurice the bike was not just a bike. It represented something important, and that something had been cruelly ripped away.

Only years later would I learn the story Maurice told me about his bicycle wasn't true. He did lose it that weekend, just not the way he said he did. Maurice was on his bicycle when he stopped to talk to some kids he knew from around the Bryant. It wasn't after dark; it was broad daylight. A man in his twenties came up and complimented him on his bike. Maurice knew the man from around the neighborhood, but they had never spoken.

"Can I take it for a spin?" the man asked.

Maurice, sitting atop his bike, said no.

"Come on, just a quick ride," the man said. "Just wanna try it out."

The man took out his wallet and handed Maurice his driver's license.

"Blood, I'm not gonna steal it," the man said. "You hold my license so you know I'm gonna bring it back."

Maurice did not want to let the man ride his bike. His instinct was to simply peddle away. But Maurice overrode that instinct; he decided to trust the man. He took the license and handed over his bike and watched the man ride off.

"I'll be back in ten minutes," the man said.

Maurice waited patiently at the corner for ten minutes. He figured the man would keep it longer; after all, it was a nifty bike. He waited half an hour, then an hour. The afternoon light gave way to evening, then to night.

Maurice waited on the corner for seven hours.

The license was fake and worthless; the bike, gone forever. Maurice felt a mix of anger and shock and sadness. Most of all, he was horrified he'd lost something I had bought for him—something I'd entrusted him with. He decided there was no way he could tell me the truth; the truth made him sound careless and stupid. Instead he told me two thugs ripped him off.

I look back now and I know why Maurice overrode his instincts. It was because of me. He had seen how I trusted him: how I'd let him into my apartment, how I never worried he'd swipe any quarters from my giant jug of change. He had heard me say there is nothing more important than trust. He had been the beneficiary of my kindness, and he was moved to extend a similar kindness to someone else. He had come to understand the concepts of trust and friendship so well that he was now ready to put them into practice.

And the person he chose to believe in ripped his heart out.

Had I, in fact, endangered Maurice by filling his mind with lofty ideas that had no relevance to his life? Was I stripping him of a protective layer he needed to survive on the streets? Had I just been fooling myself—and deceiving him—by thinking a few meals and a new bike could make any kind of difference in his world? A difficult question had to be asked: was I doing more harm than good?

Then Maurice told me about his mother being arrested—but there, again, he didn't tell me the whole story.

In the days before her arrest, Maurice was thrilled by the prospect of a new apartment. He had spent his life sharing tiny rooms with ten or twelve people, and now, for the first time, he would have a three-bedroom apartment just for his mother, his sisters, and himself. The move took away some of the sting of my announcement that I was leaving for White Plains. Though he never let on, not even for a second, that he was worried about our friendship, the truth is Maurice was shaken by my move. He was used to being abandoned by the adults in his life, and he couldn't help but think I might abandon him, too. He had come to love hanging out at my apartment, doing his homework there, having a place to clean his clothes. He had come to love spending time with me, and now I was moving on and moving away. Maurice never let me see it, but I would later learn he was terrified of losing what we had.

But at least he had his new apartment. It had taken his family years and years of moving through the system to qualify for their own place, and now their number had finally come up. Maurice waited excitedly for his mother to come home two days before the move, so he could hear more about their new home. Darcella didn't come home that Friday . . . or that Saturday. Maurice figured she was somewhere sleeping off a drug binge. She only had to be back in time for their move on Monday.

Instead, on that Monday, he found out from his grandmother that his mother had been arrested.

She'd been selling drugs at Port Authority, Manhattan's central bus station on the seedy fringes of Times Square. She was in a stairwell when another woman tried to rob her, and she beat the woman bloody. The commotion drew police to the scene, and they found bags of crack in Darcella's pockets. She was arrested and charged with possession of drugs with intent to sell and with attempted murder. Instead of moving on Monday, Maurice and his grandmother went to a courtroom in lower Manhattan. A Legal Aid Society lawyer explained that if the judge dismissed the case, they still had a chance to move to their new apartment. He would plead with the court for mercy and explain the family's dire circumstances, telling the judge about the apartment that was waiting for them and how it was their only hope to turn their lives around.

Maurice saw his mother shuffle into the courthouse in handcuffs. The lawyer told the judge that Darcella and her family had been homeless for seven years and lived in subhuman shelters, and now they finally had a chance to have a home of their own. Could the judge have mercy on this family and let them have this one chance at normalcy?

"Have you seen the woman that your client beat up?" the judge asked.

"She was just defending herself," the lawyer said.

"That's not defending yourself," the judge said. "That's malice with intent to harm."

The judge did not dismiss the case. He gave Darcella another court date and ordered her held until then. Maurice watched his mother disappear into the chambers behind the judge's bench.

His new apartment was gone now, too.

Darcella faced twenty-five years in jail for attempted murder. She accepted a plea deal for two and a half years. She was sent to Riker's Island and held in an all-female prison. Maurice never once visited her in those two and a half years. His grandmother went and his sisters, but not Maurice. He told himself he was not a person who visits people in jail.

The city found a decrepit Section 8 apartment for Maurice's grandmother on Hancock Street in Brooklyn. It was even smaller than their room at the Bryant. Maurice moved in with his sisters, an uncle, and, as the days went on, some people he didn't know. The place soon became just another drug den, another forsaken space with no food or peace or privacy. Maurice didn't tell me his mother's arrest had caused them to lose the apartment. I believed they still had it and were living there while his mother did her time. But, as he had often done before, Maurice shielded me from the more brutal truths of his life. He didn't tell me about the place on Hancock Street. And he didn't tell me that, after just a few days there, he couldn't stand to live like that anymore.

Maurice did not tell me that he left home and went to live on the streets.

After my move and his mother's arrest, Maurice and I continued to see each other on Mondays. We'd meet at a restaurant or go see a movie or play games at the arcade; he never let me know what was really happening in his life. There was no denying things were different, but we both decided to make the best of our new arrangement. As time passed, the geographical distance between us became a problem. I missed a Monday here and there, and so did he. After a while, we were down to three Mondays a month. Some months we met only twice.

But in the back of my mind, I had a secret plan. Things were going great with Michael, and within just a few months of meeting I was pretty sure he was going to ask me to marry him. We were having fun living together and spending time on his boat, and I could begin to see what a future with him would be like. That's when I hatched my plan: if Maurice's living situation ever got too crazy again, I could have him move in with me and Michael in his big four-bedroom house. I never mentioned this to Maurice or to Michael; I just kept tossing the idea around in my head. Michael was a wealthy man, and money never seemed to be a problem for him. I imagined the impact Michael could have on Maurice, both as a role model and as a kind of father figure. I dreamed of Michael offering to pay for Maurice's college education. I thought about how moving in with us would utterly transform Maurice's life.

Maurice, of course, never mentioned such a scenario, but I believe that, deep down, he dreamed about it, too.

At the very least, my secret plan helped assuage some of the guilt I felt about moving away. It was obvious my relationship with Maurice was growing more complicated. Annette and Bruce decided to move to Florida, and when Thanksgiving rolled around they were in the middle of packing up their house and couldn't host the dinner. Instead, we were all invited to the home of Annette's mother-in-law. It was one thing for me to bring Maurice with me to my sister's house, but bringing him to someone else's home wasn't always that simple. My friendship with him, I knew full well, was not something that could be easily explained. It was just not that easy to fit Maurice into every situation in my new, more cluttered life.

I agonized over the decision and got up late at night to hash it out with myself. In the end I agreed to go—without Maurice. It was, at the time, one of the hardest decisions I'd ever had to make, and just thinking about it today ties my stomach in knots. I wanted more than anything to spend Thanksgiving with Maurice, but I also wanted to be with the man I loved and with my sister and her family before they moved to Florida. Looking back, I should have simply said I wouldn't go anywhere without Maurice.

But that's not what I did. What I did was tell Maurice I wouldn't be seeing him on Thanksgiving.

And, as he had before, Maurice told me not to feel bad about it.

"Don't worry about me," he said. "We can see each other right after Thanksgiving anyway."

And, of course, we still had Christmas, our favorite holiday.

A week before Thanksgiving, Nancy got married to her fiancé, John—the guy who had been with us on my blind double date with Michael. Right after the reception, in the hotel room where Michael and I were staying, Michael handed me a small black box and asked me to marry him. It wasn't a total surprise; he'd asked me to help him pick out the ring. I had selected the diamond and the mountings and I knew it would be beautiful, but I hadn't seen it put together. When he proposed, I jumped in his arms and said yes. After my first disastrous marriage, I wasn't sure I'd ever fall in love again. And now I had, to a wonderful man, and I still had a chance to live my dream—to have a beautiful family of my own. We set a date for the following June.

Then it was time to start planning for my first Christmas with Michael in White Plains. It was a few weeks before Christmas when I mentioned to Michael that I would be inviting Maurice to join us.

Michael said, "I don't think that's appropriate."

I had to take a moment or two to let that sink in.

"What do you mean, it's not appropriate?"

"I don't think you should invite Maurice to Christmas."

"Hold on," I said. "You know Maurice is a friend of mine. You know how important he is to me. Why don't you want me to invite him?"

"Because I don't know anything about him," he said. "I don't know anything about his family."

"Maurice is a great kid. He's a friend of mine, and I will vouch for him."

"Laura, it's not that I don't trust Maurice, but he has a family. He has relatives we know nothing about, and I don't want to bring all that into our life here."

Michael and I continued the argument for hours.

I simply couldn't believe what I was hearing. I was angry, confused, in shock. It had never dawned on me that Michael would not invite Maurice into our lives. Not in a million years did I think he would ever ban him from our home. We hadn't seriously discussed it, but I had talked about Maurice a lot and he knew what our relationship was like. For me, it just went without saying that Maurice would be a part of our family. To now learn the man I dearly loved didn't share this view was completely shattering. But that wasn't the worst of it; Michael was not only against inviting Maurice to Christmas, he was *dead set* against it. He was a confident, self-possessed man, used to getting his way and not having to compromise. He simply would not budge on this matter.

"How can you be so callous?"

"What's the big deal?"

"I made a commitment to him. You know how I feel about him."

"I never said you can't see him."

"But I can't bring him to our home?"

"It wouldn't be a comfortable situation."

We argued and argued until we were both exhausted, then I got in bed and pulled the covers over my head. I tried to sleep but couldn't, and at 2:00 a.m. I got up, got dressed, drove down Mamaroneck Avenue, and parked by the water. I just sat in my car, crying. The realization that it would be hard for me to balance my friendship with Maurice and my life with Michael was one of the most painful realizations I'd ever had. As I sat in my car, I kept hearing Miss House's message to me: *Do not abandon this child.* I thought of Maurice and where he was at that moment, in a bed with dirty sheets, in a home without a mother. I thought about his bicycle being stolen; I thought about our little cookie-baking ritual that was now gone. I thought about where Maurice would go on Christmas if he couldn't be with me. A Salvation Army, a box of donated toys.

And I thought about what I could say or do to change Michael's mind. The most distressing thing was that he was so utterly unyielding. It never occurred to me that our disagreement over Maurice could damage our relationship. I was in love with Michael, and I still wanted to marry him and have children with him, but I had just seen a side of him I hadn't seen before—an intransigence, maybe even a selfishness, but certainly a disregard for the sickening anguish I felt. If he wouldn't do this for Maurice, wouldn't he want to do it for me? How could he not see his decision was breaking my heart? And if he could see it, how could he not care?

I drove home and got in bed and didn't say a word to Michael for four days.

After that, what I should have done was draw a line in the sand. I should have said Michael could not have me if he didn't accept Maurice as well. I should have said Michael's and my life did not belong just to him and his family; it belonged to both of us. Maurice was part of *our* life, like it or not. I should have said Maurice is coming for Christmas, and that's that.

But I did not say those things. Instead, once again, I met Maurice at a restaurant and told him I wouldn't be able to see him on Christmas. I promised I would see him the Monday right after Christmas, and I would bring my presents for him then, and we would get right back to seeing each other every Monday, and *I'm sorry, Maurice, I'm sorry, I'm sorry, I'm just so very sorry*, and Maurice, betraying nothing, said, "Laurie, it's okay."

The next June, Michael and I got married in a small ceremony in our home in White Plains. We invited around a hundred people, and we set up a tent in the backyard. On a beautiful summer day we said our vows not far from the brook that cut through our property. It was, by anyone's standards, a lovely wedding.

Except that my friend Maurice was not there.

16

THE WINTER COAT

One day at his grandmother's Section 8 apartment in Brooklyn, Maurice counted the number of people in the tiny room. There were twelve. Not all of them lived there, but they were there a lot—cousins, uncles, friends, drug connections, people from the neighborhood, addicts sleeping it off. This was the way Maurice lived: fighting for space in a filthy room. But after his mother was sent to prison—after he lost the one person he loved most of all—Maurice couldn't take the craziness anymore. And so he just left.

Maurice knew the streets well. Big dining rooms and giant jugs of quarters and gift-wrapped presents might baffle him, but the streets were something he understood in and out. He'd grown at least three inches since I'd met him, and he was tall for his age, lean and strong—closer now to being a man than a boy. He was confident in his ability to survive off the grid; he knew how to scrounge for meals and elude cops and act tough when he had to. And, at least two or three times a month, he could still meet me in the city. Those meetings, I found out, were more important for Maurice than ever. They were the only dose of normalcy in a world that was becoming increasingly hostile to him.

Maurice knew where he would sleep—at the rundown Kung Fu Theater on 42nd Street in Times Square. It was officially known as the Times Square Theater, but they ran kung fu movies around the clock. Maurice would panhandle the money for a ticket, find a seat in the back, curl up there, and sleep through the night, the shrill cracks of kung fu fights filling his head. During the day he'd panhandle for more ticket money and go to the theater across the street to watch the Eddie Murphy movie *Coming to America* over and over again. He must have seen it three hundred times. He knew all the dialogue by heart.

He'd sneak into the YMCA on West 59th Street to steal a shower, and every once in a while he'd go back to Brooklyn to check on his grandmother. He never stayed long, and no one asked where he was going or where he slept. For a while he still attended I.S. 131, but eventually he was moved to another school—an alternative school. He didn't know what that meant until he noticed most of the students had profound mental and emotional problems. He didn't feel he belonged, and after just a few months he stopped going. By the time he was sixteen, he was done with school altogether.

The challenge for Maurice now was to find a way to make money. He didn't want to panhandle anymore. There was an obvious solution, a blindingly apparent and available option: he could, like nearly every other man in his life, sell drugs. There was nothing else that would earn him anywhere near the amount of money he could make from selling crack. He'd seen how lucrative the business was, watched his uncles peel off twenties and hundreds from fat rolls of bills. And he knew how to do it: knew where to buy the drugs, how to cut them, where to sell them. He could have walked into the drug trade in a second and made hundreds of dollars his first day. When he was homeless and living in a movie theater, he thought about it—thought about it long and hard. He was fighting himself and trying to find a reason he shouldn't give in to the call and the cash of crack.

But something held him back. Something told him it was a dead-end choice. Instead, Maurice walked into a messenger agency in midtown Manhattan. These were agencies that hired young men and teenagers to ferry packages from company to company on foot. The first agency sent Maurice away, and the second, and the third, but he kept at it. Finally, Bullet Messenger Manpower agreed to give him a try. Maurice picked up files and letters and legal documents and ran them across town, into subways, and up and down the island of Manhattan, making around eight dollars an hour. He gave up panhandling for good.

Maurice liked getting a paycheck and cashing it and having money he'd earned with good, hard work. He liked the money so much, he wanted more. He'd seen how it takes smarts and energy to be successful at selling drugs, and he knew he had both. He knew he could outhustle anyone on the streets. He knew he could master the salesmanship: the buying and selling and moving of merchandise. So he got in the business of selling—not drugs, but blue jeans.

Maurice would go to Chinatown and buy knockoff Guess jeans for seven dollars a pair, then resell them for as much as forty dollars. This was the late '80s, and the bootleg jeans business was burgeoning in New York City. At first he sold the jeans to other messengers, then branched out to drug dealers and their girlfriends. He found he could make several hundred dollars a week selling jeans. Every few days he went to Brooklyn and gave some of the money to his grandmother, so she could buy food and take care of herself. He didn't tell her where he got the money, and she didn't ask. Maurice knew that selling fake jeans was illegal, but he was homeless, destitute, and uncertain about his future. Under those circumstances, drawing a clear line between right and wrong is not always a simple thing to do. The imperative for Maurice was to stay alive and to make enough money to help his family; under that pressure, the choice he made—to sell blue jeans instead of crack cocaine—was, to him, the right and reasonable choice.

After a while, Maurice made enough to move out of the Kung Fu Theater. He began renting a room for forty-five dollars a night at a cheap hotel—the kind of place that rented by the hour, mostly to hookers and johns. It was dirty and noisy and dangerous, but to Maurice it was something else as well.

It was the first time in his life he had his own room, his own bed, his own shower.

In this way, Maurice survived. At one point, he checked into Covenant House, a home for wayward and runaway youth in Times Square, but Maurice didn't like it there and quickly checked out. He even did something that was once unthinkable, he walked into the offices of the Bureau of Child Welfare. He hoped they'd send him to a group home for boys where at least he'd get meals and a bed and a chance to figure things out. Instead, they pored through his files and discovered they'd once entrusted him to his grandmother's care. They found out where she lived and sent Maurice right back to where he started.

So Maurice went right back out on the street.

And then his mother came home. She was released from prison after two and a half years, and the city assigned her a spot in a shelter in the tough Brownsville section of Brooklyn. Darcella was then given a two-room apartment, which meant Maurice could move in with her. And that's what he did. It was just the two of them—his older sisters had moved in with boyfriends—and it was the best living arrangement Maurice had ever had. His mother was clean, at least for a while, and there were no cousins or uncles or drug fiends crowding them out. It was just Darcella and Maurice, a mother and her son.

Until the day Maurice came home and saw a short, skinny man sitting in the kitchen talking to his mother.

"Who's that?" Maurice asked her.

"That's your father," she said.

He hadn't seen his father since he was six years old—the day his mother showed up with a hammer to bring him home. That summer, Morris had asked to have his son live with him, and, for whatever reason, Darcella agreed. In those three months, Maurice nearly died of malnutrition. He developed ringworm and lost so much weight his ribs showed through his skin. His father's gross neglect may have proved fatal, but Darcella arrived just in time and chased away Morris and his girlfriend with a hammer, taking her boy back home. After that, Maurice's father disappeared from his life. Now, many years later, he was back.

Maurice couldn't believe how weak and frail his father was. The swagger and fearsomeness was gone; now he just looked old. Even so, the bad memories were still there, and Maurice wasn't happy to see him.

"What's he doin' here?" he asked his mother. "Get him out."

With that, Maurice turned and left, saying nothing to his father.

Not much later he heard through the streets that Morris had AIDS. Maybe he had contracted it through a dirty needle, maybe unprotected sex. Maurice would see his father on the street and steer clear of him, but he couldn't help but feel sorry for him, too. Morris was once the most powerful man he knew, scared of no one, a terror to all, and here he was shuffling around like a man twice his age. One day Maurice saw his father stumble and fall on the sidewalk. Without thinking, he ran and helped him up. After that, they spoke every once in a while, which gave Maurice the chance to ask the question he'd always wanted to ask: "Man, why did you have to be that way? I should have wanted to be just like you, but you made me want to be nothing like you. Why'd you have to be that way?"

His father, his voice a near whisper, said, "It was the only way I knew."

And then he apologized, over and over. "I'm sorry, son," he said. "Don't you know how sorry I am? Don't ever be like me. I don't want you to be like me."

Maurice watched his father get weaker and skinnier. Toward the end, he ran into Maurice on the street and stopped him for a talk.

"I know I never did much of anything for you, but there's one thing I want you to do for me."

Maurice braced himself for the request.

"The one thing I ask of you," he said, "is that you name your son Maurice."

Maurice had always hated his name, because it had been his father's name and his father's name before that. He knew he would never give his own son that name, not in a million years. But the old man was sick and Maurice felt compassion, so he said to his father, "Yeah, okay, I will."

A few days later, a neighbor told Maurice that his father had died that morning. It was Halloween day. Maurice went to the apartment where his father had been staying and found him lying on the floor beside a mattress. Maurice bent down and picked up his father, laying him on the bed. He was startled by how light he was. The toughest guy in Brooklyn, the king of the Tomahawks, was now just skin and bones. Maurice waited until an ambulance arrived. He watched the EMTs take his father away. Then he left the apartment and walked into the street.

At the time it happened, Maurice didn't tell me his father had died. He was shielding me, as he usually did, from a sad and difficult chapter in his life, but the complex emotions he had for his father—the ragged, scarring, unfinished nature of their relationship—was something I would have been able to relate to. I could grasp as well as anyone how a muddied family history could impact us as adults—how the things we carry with us from childhood define who we become.

Aside from our disagreements about Maurice—and that was no small thing—Michael and I were doing well as a married couple. Michael never said I couldn't have Maurice in my life, and I kept seeing him. Eventually, Michael came with me to see him, and the three of us shared many meals and outings. Michael could see Maurice was special and finally began to understand why he was so important to me. He even relented and allowed me to invite Maurice to our home for Christmas one year. Nancy and her husband and Steven came up, too, and we all had a wonderful time—but it just wasn't like the old days at Annette's house. I still cannot say Michael ever bonded with Maurice in any meaningful way; he always kept a wall up between them. I was happy to have Maurice in our lives as much as he was, but it became painfully clear that my dream of having him move in with us was never going to happen. I never even brought it up.

Michael's stubbornness worried me on another front, too. I was over forty years old now, and my window for having a baby was closing. Having children was not something Michael and I had specifically discussed before we got married, and, in hindsight, that was a terrible mistake. At the time, I was having so much fun with him and was so wrapped up in the romance that it didn't occur to me to sit him down and have that conversation. I knew he loved me, and I assumed that's what people who love each other do—have kids. I didn't think it was going to be an issue.

So it was more than a year into our marriage when I finally sat him down and had the talk.

"I want to have a family," I said. "I want to have children."

Michael looked down at the floor, then back up at me.

"I'm not interested in having another kid," he said.

I'd expected a little hemming and hawing, but his matter-of-fact tone, his decisiveness, was a shock. I told him how important it was to me to have children and what a great mother I was going to be, and wasn't he even a little interested in seeing what our child would be like?

"Not even in the slightest," he said.

He had two grown sons and loved them dearly. He was fiercely proud of them, but in his mind he was done raising children and that was that. I told him I would do all the work. I told him I'd get up for all the feedings. I told him I'd pay for a nanny—anything to make it as easy as possible. But Michael, as he had been about Maurice, didn't budge. I kept at him, kept bringing it up; in about our thirtieth argument he finally laid down the law.

"It's not up for discussion, Laura," he said. "I'm absolutely not going to do it."

I shrank away from him, defeated. I took my wound, nursed it as best I could, and I waited for it to heal and disappear. But what caused that wound remained as a source of pain. Over time that pain turned into resentment, and I tried to push that resentment down as far as it would go so I could keep on living. But it stayed there, below the surface but not that far down at all.

And so I slowly let go of my dream. I'd always wanted to have two children, because I never wanted my son or daughter to be an only child. When I turned forty-two, I realized I'd all but run out of time to have two kids. Even if I could somehow miraculously convince Michael to change his mind, I'd probably only be able to have one child. It struck me that this would be selfish—that I'd be thinking only about myself and not about the child. I don't remember when exactly it happened. Maybe there wasn't a single moment, or day, or week. But over time, the dream that for years had been a nearly consuming passion simply ceased to be.

All of our stories, as much as they are about anything, are about loss. And, perhaps, they are about what might have been. I wanted happy, loving parents who danced waltzes in the living room. I wanted children of my own, desperately. We all want relationships that are healthy and resolved, and sometimes that simply doesn't happen. But the beauty of life is that inside these disappointments are hidden the most miraculous of blessings. What we lose and what might have been pales against what we have.

I think back to my own father and how contentious our relationship was. He had dominated my childhood, but as an adult I refused to let him hold the same power over me. I had essentially cut him off. At the same time I felt bad about leaving my sisters and brothers to take care of him as he got older. I didn't want to skip out on that responsibility. So I'd go back to Long Island at least once or twice a month to see him and help tidy up the house and do anything I could to help Nancy, who tended to most of my father's needs, and Steven, who was still living at home and had to bear the brunt of my father's bitterness.

In the spring of 1987 I drove to Long Island and cleaned my

father's house from top to bottom. I did laundry, folded sheets, picked up stray cigarette butts. I was nearly finished when he came home from somewhere. There were times when he'd be happy to see me and everything would be great, but if he was angry about anything, he'd do what he always did: curse, criticize, belittle. On this day, he immediately started picking on me. I can't remember what he said; I think I've blocked it out. I was tired and irritable, and finally I lost control and let my father have it.

"You've been nothing but a bully your whole life," I told him, rising up into a fury. "You bullied mom, and that's why she died of cancer. You bullied Frank, and that's why he stutters and his life is so hard. You constantly abuse all of us, and I'm sick and tired of it. I'm not going to put up with it anymore!"

My father was shocked into silence. I walked out the door and never spoke to my father again.

About a year and a half later, only a few weeks after I turned thirty-eight, Annette called me to let me know he was really sick. He hadn't been well in a while, and he was getting weaker. We had to get Meals on Wheels to bring food to the house for him. His doctors told him to stop smoking, but he never did. Even when he was hooked up to an oxygen tank at home, he still found a way to smoke; the Meals on Wheels volunteers refused to go into our house because they were afraid it would blow up. Then my father's breathing became labored, and my sisters took him to a hospital. They called me to let me know Dad was getting worse. I did not go see him, and my sisters and brothers understood why. However, they worried that if I didn't see him before he died, I'd be filled with remorse. I told them I was okay with my decision, and they never pushed me.

Annette spent the most time with him at the hospital. She was there the day his breathing got raspy and my father sputtered, "I am going to die." But his breathing had been bad before, and he'd said that many times. The nurses told my sister she should go home and come back in the morning.

Later that day, they called her and told her he had taken a turn for the worse. She rushed back to the hospital, but by the time she got there our father had died. He had died alone with none of his children there, and I couldn't help but think of my mother's final hours, how all of us surrounded her holding her hands and telling her how much we loved her. To this day I cannot say I regret not speaking to my father in his last months on earth. I know that may sound callous to some, but it is the truth. I do feel tremendous sadness that he died alone. I feel sadness, because I know the kind of father he could have been.

None of his children knew what to say at his funeral. Finally, it was Steven, the youngest, who wrote an obituary for him and read it at the mass. Steven, then twenty-five, talked about how my father loved *The Honeymooners,* and how, like the show, he had his own devoted followers—the people who drank in his bars. He talked about my father's time at the Picture Lounge and the bowling alley bar and at Funzy's Tavern and how everywhere he went he made new friends. "He wasn't just a bartender; he was more than that," Steven said. "He had a great memory for faces. He had a knack for remembering drinks. And he had the gift of gab." It was a beautiful speech and it made all of us cry, and it was 100 percent true. My father *was* a wonderful man—we just didn't get to see him be that as much as we should have.

Years later Steven told me that in one of his last conversations with my father, he asked him why he acted the way he did.

"I don't know," my father said. "I don't mean to yell at you. I am sorry that I was the way I was."

My father apologized to Steven many times that day and, in that way, apologized to us all. I already knew he was sorry about the things he did, and I knew he couldn't change who he was. I know, too, that he loved my mother, more deeply than he could have ever hoped to show her. I told myself that in heaven my father wouldn't be able to torment my mother anymore. In heaven, he wouldn't be broken. In heaven, maybe he and my mother would dance those waltzes after all.

One year after his father died, Maurice met a girl named Meka. One of his uncles was dating her mother, and they'd see each other all the time. He didn't like her at first; he thought she was too loud, too argumentative. He could see she had a sweet side, but mainly she liked to fight, and Maurice had had enough fighting in his life. One night Meka leaned over and kissed him. He said, "I don't like you that way." But she didn't give up, and soon enough Maurice was feeling something he'd never felt before.

I remember Michael and I took Maurice and Meka to dinner. She was very sweet and told me she loved to read. There were things about her I really liked, but she was so young, like Maurice, and I left that dinner feeling pretty worried. I was afraid she'd get pregnant, and I couldn't imagine Maurice having to raise a child. Later, I asked him to promise me he would be careful, and he did. But I couldn't shake a nagging feeling that something might happen.

Maurice's life was actually fairly stable at that point. His mother had gone back to using drugs, but she wasn't nearly as hardcore as before. As soon as Maurice turned eighteen, he was eligible to apply for a Section 8 apartment of his own. His mother was no longer eligible—her prison sentence had taken care of that—but here was a way for Maurice to finally help his mother. He could get an apartment and let Darcella live there. He filled out all the paperwork, and, on one of the greatest days of his life, a city official handed him the keys to a two-bedroom apartment on Hillside Avenue. Maurice walked through the front door, dropped to his knees, and kissed the floor.

He hadn't had a proper home in ten years. And now he had one.

Maurice moved his mother into the apartment while he stayed with Meka in Brooklyn. He and Meka fought a lot, but they also had their share of fun. They liked going to Coney Island, and Maurice was proud of the giant stuffed white teddy bear he won there in a game. The day he found out Meka was pregnant was another one of the great days of his life. He had never thought about having children, never pictured himself bouncing a son on his knee, but now that he was facing fatherhood he felt nothing but elation. He didn't know why it meant so much to him to have a child. He just knew that it did.

Maurice was there at St. Vincent's Hospital in downtown Manhattan when Meka gave birth to a healthy baby boy. He held his tiny, gnarled son and kissed him on the forehead. Earlier he'd told Meka what he'd like to name his son, and she told him she liked the name and it was fine with her.

And so that night, he held his firstborn son, Maurice.

The next day he left the hospital and took the subway to his apartment to see his mother. She was living there with his sister LaToya and her young son; his sister Celeste's young daughter was visiting. Maurice turned the corner, looked up at his apartment, and stopped dead in his tracks.

All he saw was charred, smoldering holes where the windows once were.

Maurice ran upstairs, terrified for his family. His apartment had been gutted in a fire. He asked neighbors about his mother, but no one knew what had happened. Only later that day did Maurice discover his mother and sister and niece and nephew were safe and sound. He also found out what had caused the fire.

His niece and nephew had been playing with a lighter and set fire to Maurice's giant white teddy bear; the apartment went up in flames.

In an instant, Maurice was homeless again.

When Maurice told me he had a son, I was not happy at all. Of course I knew he was going to have children some day, but he was only nineteen and I felt he was too young, too unsettled, to have a child of his own. I told him it was irresponsible to bring a baby into the world, given his circumstances, and how terrified I was that the cycle that had consumed his parents and nearly consumed him was now starting again. Maurice understood how I felt, and all he told me was that he would be okay.

"Don't worry, Laurie. I got this," he said.

Because of my reaction, he didn't ask me to come see his new son, nor did he bring him around when we met in the city. I wish I could have been happier for him and more supportive, but I just couldn't. I was worried the responsibility of having a son might push Maurice into making bad decisions. I was also having a hard time seeing Maurice as a full-grown man. I had met him only eight years earlier when he was just a child himself. And here he was, a father, charged with raising a child of his own. To be honest, the thought of that terrified me. I believed in Maurice and I knew he was special, but I felt that whatever gains he had made since meeting me were fragile. Not because of him, but because of the world he lived in.

I wonder, also, if my own baby issues had something to do with my reaction. This was right around the time it was becoming clear to me that I would never have children of my own. Something I had wanted more desperately than anything else was slipping away, and there was nothing I could do about it. And here was Maurice, too young to be a father, not ready for the responsibility, having a son at nineteen. Did some part of me resent how cavalierly he seemed to be approaching fatherhood? Was I mad at God for how unfair it seemed? Perhaps.

What helped me deal with it was seeing how thrilled Maurice was to be a father. He told me he wanted his son to have all the things he never had and to never know the kind of troubles he had faced every day. I could see Maurice's face light up whenever he talked about his son. He called him Junior and showed me pictures, and he promised over and over that he would be a good father to his boy. I realized that if I believed in Maurice, I had to believe in him through even the most difficult of times. I had to let Maurice live his own life.

Sometime after his son's fourth birthday, Maurice and I got together in Manhattan. Christmas was coming up, and the winter air was thin and cold. Maurice and I talked about Meka and about Junior and about how he was doing.

Then Maurice did something he had never done before.

He asked to borrow money.

He said Meka had seen a winter coat she loved, and he wanted to buy it for her. He said the coat cost three hundred dollars.

"Maurice, that's pretty expensive for a coat," I said.

"But she saw it and she really likes it, and I want to get it for her," he said.

I had never even considered what I would do if Maurice asked me for money. I thought back to when I had given him the choice between cash and brown bag lunches and he had chosen the lunches hands down. I'd spent thousands and thousands of dollars on Maurice, but our relationship had never been about money. I was taken aback that he was asking for money now.

I'd also been feeling guilty about spending less time with him and about how I had reacted to his son, and so I told him I'd make him a deal.

"I will give you two hundred dollars outright, but I will loan you the other hundred. You have to start paying me back immediately. I don't care if it's a quarter a week, but you have to pay me back. Do you understand, Maurice?"

"Absolutely," he said. "And thank you so much, Laurie."

We walked to an ATM, I pulled out three hundred dollars, and he hugged me and thanked me again. Then we went our separate ways.

The next Monday, when we were set to get together, I didn't hear from Maurice. I didn't hear from him the Monday after that. A month went by, then another.

And just like that, Maurice disappeared from my life.

17

THE DARK FOREST

In the eight years since I'd met Maurice, the longest we'd ever gone without talking or seeing each other was three weeks. We'd each become an automatic part of the other's routine, and our conversations and outings were, at least to me, integral to my life. Now, all of a sudden, he was gone. I knew Maurice lived in Brooklyn, but I didn't have his address—he'd always kept me away from wherever he lived, preferring just to meet me in Manhattan. And I didn't have a phone number for him. This was still before cell phones, and I wasn't even sure he had a landline. After I moved to White Plains, Maurice would always call me at my office on Mondays to confirm we were getting together. I could always count on hearing from him sooner or later.

But now, nothing. He'd been missing for eight months when my birthday rolled around, and I was sure I'd hear from him then. Since I'd met him, he'd never forgotten to call me and wish me a happy birthday. But that day passed, too, with no word. I started poring through phone books and calling every Mazyck I could find, to no avail. Thanksgiving, then Christmas, then another birthday, and still nothing. I told my assistant Rachel at *Teen People* magazine, where I was working, that if anyone named Maurice should call, she should find me and put it through immediately. On the streets of Manhattan I'd think I had seen him on a corner or in a bus, but it was never him. I had to face the possibility that Maurice could be out of my life for good. I even started worrying he might be dead.

Looking back now, the story of what happened to Maurice brings to mind one of the great themes of mythology—what Joseph Campbell called the hero's journey. It is a voyage many of us have had to make in one way or another. It happens on our path to discovering who we are and what we are made of. When we are young and full of energy but still naïve about the world, we are lured into a dark, mysterious forest—a forest that seduces us with the promise of great things. There we face challenges more intense than we could have fathomed, and how we fare in those challenges determines who we become. If we make it out of the forest alive, we are wiser and stronger, and the gifts we bring back with us will make the world a better place. The hero's journey is a journey of self-discovery.

Maurice disappeared from my life so that he could enter that dark forest.

Maurice's voyage began with a betrayal. He knew his father had done drugs, and of course he knew his mother was an addict. He knew all his uncles and practically every other adult in his life were involved in drugs. But there was one person who hadn't been sucked into the vortex, one person who, through it all, had stayed clean. And that was Maurice's grandmother, Rose.

Maurice believed for most of his young life that Grandma Rose did not do drugs. She was the one who kept everything together while his mother was out scoring or in jail. She was the one who would comfort Maurice, tell him what a good boy he was, and tell him not to worry, that his mother would be home soon because she loved him more than anything. His grandmother was the rock in their crazy family. When he was young, Maurice noticed his grandmother never slept at night—she just stayed up in her chair—and he asked her why.

"Because I gotta watch out for my kids," she'd say. "I'm always watching over you."

Maurice believed that was true. His grandmother was his protector.

Then, around the time his son was born, Maurice learned his grandmother had cancer and was in a hospital for treatment. That by itself was a terrible blow, but then Maurice heard one of his aunts say Rose had asked for a bag of dope.

"What are you talking about?" Maurice asked her. "What would she be doing with a bag of dope?"

His aunt told him Rose did drugs all the time.

Maurice was crushed. Slowly, he put the pieces together: the reason she stayed up all night was to do her drugs without the children seeing. In the mornings she'd nod off and sleep during the day. Maurice felt angry and betrayed, and he rushed to the hospital to confront his grandmother. He got there too early for visiting hours, but he'd been in the hospital before and knew his way around. He snuck in through the basement and went to the fifth floor. He walked into Rose's room and found her in bed, hooked to a respirator, but her oxygen mask had come off and her gown was filthy. It looked to Maurice like no one was taking care of her, and he started yelling for a doctor or nurse, demanding they come and take care of his grandmother. Instead, two security guards grabbed Maurice, subdued him, and ushered him out of the hospital.

His grandmother died that night. He never got to talk to her.

He carried the betrayal with him for a while, but over time he realized his grandmother hadn't betrayed him at all. Yes, she had succumbed to drugs, but she had kept her addiction a secret from Maurice so that he could see the best in her. And she *had* been his protector; she *had* steered him away from drugs, ever since the day she handed him that joint and then took it away. She had seen something special in Maurice, and she had done everything she could to keep him safe, right up to the day she died.

But now, she was gone. She could not be his protector anymore. That's when Maurice realized he was no longer the one who needed protection.

He had a family now, and he had to become a protector for them.

In fact, his family was growing. Four months after Junior was born, Maurice and Meka split up; they simply fought too much to make it work. Maurice had seen his parents spend all their time fighting, and he didn't want that for Junior. They agreed to raise Junior together, even though they were apart. Then Maurice met a beautiful girl named Michelle and fell in love. Michelle liked that Maurice was quiet and reserved—that he didn't need to be seen and heard like all the other noisy boys she knew. He saw the same quality in her—she was smart, centered, sure of herself. And Michelle had a tough exterior—quick to fight and slow to trust. For her, compromising meant ceding control, and that was something she'd never do. Maurice sat her down and told her, "I'm not always going to have everything you want, but if you stick with me you will always have everything you need. Ride out the tough times with me and trust me, and we will make it together."

Michelle looked into his eyes and said, "I got you."

"I got you," Maurice said.

They moved into an apartment on Washington Avenue in Brooklyn, and they had a son they named Jalique.

Maurice did not tell me about Jalique when he was born. He had seen how I reacted to Junior's birth, and he couldn't bring himself to tell me he'd had another child. When he had borrowed the money from me, it wasn't to buy a coat for Meka.

It was to buy two winter coats, for Junior and Jalique.

What upset Maurice during that time was the feeling he was letting me down. He believed I felt he was irresponsible, and I guess I did. I wish I could go back and not be as hard on him. I didn't know my feelings would bother him as much as they did. Perhaps I should have known, but I didn't. One of the reasons he didn't call me was because he couldn't bear to be a disappointment to me.

The other reason was his realization that he needed to find a way to support his new family. He wasn't the little kid who ate steak and cookies with me any longer; he was a father now. He knew he couldn't depend on me, or anyone else, to feed him or clothe him or otherwise support him. He had to find a way to do it on his own. That's when he made a difficult decision: he was going to temporarily leave his family and go to North Carolina to try to set up a business.

Maurice's plan was to bring jeans and other clothing with him from the city to sell in North Carolina, which was a couple of steps behind New York in terms of fashion. If he could set up a pipeline, all he'd have to do is send the clothing down and get money sent back to him in New York. Michelle was dead set against the trip; she didn't like who he was going with. Maurice was traveling with two people he knew who were in the drug business, and Michelle was afraid they were going to North Carolina to sell drugs. She trusted Maurice and didn't believe he would ever sell drugs himself, but both Maurice and Michelle knew that being around bad people could lead to as much trouble as being a bad person. *Nothing good could come of this trip*, Michelle thought, and she begged Maurice not to go.

But Maurice felt it was something he had to do, so he kissed his sons good-bye, told Michelle he loved her, and got on a Greyhound bus heading south.

He went to Raleigh and Fayetteville, Greensboro and Clinton. He missed Michelle and the children and called home whenever he could, promising he'd be home soon. He didn't tell Michelle things weren't going well in North Carolina. The men he was traveling with were getting in trouble with drug dealers and local girls and their boyfriends. There were constant fights and threats. Maurice found that, try as he might to steer clear of trouble, he often found himself right in the middle of it. He'd seen how his father acted in such situations, had seen Uncle Limp and Uncle Dark being tough when they needed to be, and so his instinct was to stand and fight—to be the tough guy from New York who could handle the local gangsters. He'd been taught to prove to people that he wasn't a chump. And as long as he was around a bad element, he would have to keep on proving it.

For a while he stayed in a run-down trailer with a man named Crickett. He noticed Crickett owned a lot of guns. When he saw them, Maurice knew he didn't belong in that trailer. He was starting to realize this kind of life wasn't for him. One morning he went to a service at the local Pentecostal church, and afterward the preacher came up to him and pulled him out of the crowd.

"Son, I don't know what you're doing here, but the Lord said, 'It is time for you to go home.' He has some work for you to do. Go home."

Maurice shrugged him off. He still had business to take care of.

"If you don't leave tonight," the preacher continued, "there will be dire consequences. Your place is at home."

That night, while sitting in the trailer with Crickett and his friends, Maurice heard the screech of cars pulling up. Earlier, one of the men Maurice had come down with had fought with a local woman, and now the woman's brothers and cousins were there to set things straight. Maurice heard yelling and cursing and pounding on the trailer, and as soon as he stepped outside, he heard the first gunshot.

He dove behind a parked car and huddled against the front tire. He heard a bullet whiz past him; another shattered the windshield. The gunshots were impossibly loud, so loud he could barely think.

He saw Crickett and his friends shooting back, ducking and firing and ducking again. Maurice prayed for the shooting to stop, but it just kept going—a hundred gunshots ringing in the night.

Then Crickett tossed a gun toward Maurice.

Maurice's father would have picked up the gun, and his uncles would have, too. Now, it seemed, it was his turn. Maurice stayed close to the tire and thought about what the preacher had told him: "dire consequences." He thought about Michelle waiting for him in Brooklyn. He thought about his son Junior and his son Jalique and how when he held them in his arms he felt like more of a man than when he did anything else.

And he thought about me.

There wasn't time during the gunfight to think about all the ways that I had nagged him. *Don't be late. Punctuality is important. Smoking is bad. Do your homework. Sit up straight. Clean your clothes. Be polite.* There wasn't time to reflect on the trips to Annette's house and the dinners at the Hard Rock and the warm cookies. There was no chance to remember the moment when he told me he loved me and realized that I loved him, too. With the shrill blast of bullets echoing in his ears, he could not think back to the first baseball game he and I went to, or forward to the first game he and his sons would see together.

In the chaos and the hail of bullets, with a loaded gun at his feet, Maurice could only form four words in his head: *This is not me.*

He never picked up the gun. After twenty seconds that seemed more like twenty hours, the shooting stopped and the shooters drove away. Crickett looked down at Maurice in disgust.

"Why you crying?" he demanded.

"I have kids at home," Maurice said. "I'm leaving."

At dawn he was on a bus headed back to New York City.

Maurice walked into his apartment, saw Michelle and his boys, and said a small prayer of thanks. He wasn't sure he'd ever felt anything sweeter than the feeling of his children tugging on his body as they tried to climb up and hug him.

He was also happy to see his mother again. He'd thought of her often when he was away and worried about her, because by then Maurice knew that his mother was sick. Not long after she had finished her long prison sentence, she sat Maurice down and gave him some bad news.

She told him she had HIV.

Maurice was devastated to hear this. All he knew about HIV was that it was a death sentence. Right then and there he started preparing himself for the day his mother would die. He played the day out in his head and tried to envision how he would feel, steeling himself so that he'd be ready when it finally came.

What made her disease even harder to accept was that, after a brief relapse, Maurice's mother had kicked drugs once and for all. She'd checked in to an intense in-patient detox program, and Maurice didn't hear a word from her for three months. After that she'd spent another nine months in the St. Christopher's rehab clinic in the Bronx. Maurice visited her there and saw that she was lucid and clear-eyed and alive in a way she hadn't ever been. All the needles and the crack rocks, all the dealers and the cops, all the nights with his mother slumped in a chair, eyes rolled back in her head—all of that, a lifetime of it, was now finally behind her.

"I don't want that anymore," Darcella had said.

For Maurice, her sobriety was something close to a miracle. She doted on his children, told stories to Junior, sang songs to Jalique, took them to the Big Apple Circus, thrilled them with her affection and attention. And Maurice was thrilled by it, too. One of his favorite memories is of his first birthday after his mother got clean. He had a party. His children were there, and his sisters and cousins and his mother, too, laughing and singing and having fun. *This is what birthday parties are supposed to be like,* he thought. *This is nice. This is good.*

Maurice had always known his mother loved him. He knew that from the day she showed up with a hammer to get him back. He knew she'd done the best she could to shield him from her drug use. He never once felt she had let him down or failed him in any way. She had a sickness, that was true, a sickness that gripped her like the devil himself. But even in the face of that she had kept her family together, and now her son had a family of his own. Maurice did not feel cheated one bit, only blessed.

Then one day in 2000, Maurice got a call from LaToya. She told him she hadn't seen their mother in days. Maurice panicked. He was sure she hadn't slipped back into drugs. He was *positive* she hadn't. Later that day he got a call from an attendant at Woodhull Medical and Mental Health Center in Brooklyn. His mother had suffered a stroke and collapsed in the street, and when paramedics got to her, she was in cardiac arrest. Now she was in a coma.

Maurice sat with her in her hospital room every day. She came in and out of consciousness and sometimes she opened her eyes and moved her arms, but she was on a respirator and could not talk. So

Maurice did the talking for her. He told her she should feel proud of her children. Her daughters were doing well and had families of their own. She knew he had a family, too, and she knew he was going to make something of himself.

He read to her from the scriptures—Psalm 51:

Have mercy upon me, O God, according to thy loving kindness: according unto the multitude of thy tender mercies blot out my transgressions.
Wash me thoroughly from mine iniquity, and cleanse me from my sin.

Maurice left the Bible open to Psalm 51 and placed it by his mother in her bed. He left believing she was getting better and was only a few days away from joining him and his family again.

But that night, at 4:00 a.m., he got a phone call. His mother had passed away.

Maurice was asked to identify her body at the hospital. He didn't want to do it, but he knew he had to. When he saw his mother's body, he was surprised by how he felt. He felt liberated. His mother looked natural and peaceful, as if all the burdens she had carried for so long had been lifted. Maurice bent down and hugged and kissed her. He said his final good-bye.

Just a few days after that, I was in my office in the Time & Life Building when my assistant Rachel poked her head into my office, excited to tell me Maurice was on the phone.

"Oh my God," I said aloud. "Put him through."

It had been about three and a half years since I had heard from Maurice. I had no idea where he had gone or what had happened to him. My heart was beating wildly when I picked up the phone.

"Maurice? Is that you?"

"Laurie," he said, and I could tell he was crying.

"Maurice, are you okay? Is everything okay?"

"My mother died," he told me. He explained how she had gotten clean and then had a stroke, and how he had identified her body. He told me that he felt sad that she was dead but happy that she was at peace.

And then he said, "Laurie, you are my mother now."

18

ONE LAST TEST

Maurice called me right after coming home from his mother's funeral. He told me he'd thought of calling me many times over the years he was missing but just never did. For one thing, he felt bad about the hundred dollars he owed me.

"Maurice, how could you ever think a hundred dollars would mean more to me than you do?" I exclaimed. "I was worried sick about you."

"I'm so sorry," he told me. "I just had to go away and figure things out."

He told me that after his mother died he thought about how, in his life, there had been only a handful of people who truly cared for him. He lost one of them when his grandmother died and another when his mother passed away. After that, he said, he couldn't stand to lose one more. And so he finally called me.

We scheduled a time to get together the next day, and we met at a restaurant to catch up with each other's lives. When I saw Maurice, he looked older, more mature; he was a man now. But his big, broad smile was just the same as I remembered it, the same as on that very first day at McDonald's. Maurice told me about his mother losing her Section 8 apartment. He told me about his children, and he told me how, in North Carolina, he had faced a fork in the road between the two paths his life could take. In North Carolina, he'd come the closest he ever had to tumbling down the wrong path. Yet here he was, swearing he would never put himself in such a situation again.

"I know what's at stake now," he said. "I don't ever want to risk losing what matters to me in the world."

Seeing Maurice again and hearing him talk, I felt an enormous wave of relief pass over me. I felt like he'd turned a very big corner. In life, there are many different kinds of heroes, but sometimes you can be something more than a hero.

You can be a survivor.

Maurice understood that surviving the childhood he had endured, surviving the streets where he grew up and still lived, was by no means a given—in fact, it was a long shot. That is hardly an exaggeration. Just look at what happened to Maurice's uncles.

Uncle Limp's body broke down from years of drug abuse. He is now badly hobbled by diabetes and in prison on a parole violation.

Uncle Juice slowly lost his mind from drugs. He is still on the streets selling perfume.

Uncle Old just finished a ten-year stretch in prison for bank robbery.

Uncle Nice is in a federal penitentiary, serving ten years for drug trafficking.

Uncle E died of AIDS.

Uncle Dark is still out there somewhere on the streets. No one knows.

There were other casualties. At least five children Maurice grew up around at the Brooklyn Arms became drug addicts. He knows of at least three cousins who went to prison. One close cousin, who was the same age as Maurice and grew up with him at the Brooklyn Arms, went to jail on drug charges and, when he got out, was shot and killed.

For many of these doomed people in Maurice's life, there was simply no escape from the heavy, burdensome weight of the past. That burden is something I am sure many, many people understand, and it is something I understand pretty well, too. I know that struggling against the vicious undertow of inherited sadness—the ever-present pull of family history—can be a lifelong battle that is never won, only endured.

For some, the battle is fated to end in tragedy.

My brother Frank had been such a good athlete as a kid, I often wonder if he might have had a career as a professional athlete. He was great at baseball, great at wrestling; he was even a champion bowler. His room was full of shiny trophies, little gold men swinging bats or crouched in wrestling poses. His love of sports was one of the few things that might have allowed him to bond with my father. He always said his fondest childhood memory was when my father came home from work one day and gave him two tickets to see his favorite team, the Minnesota Twins, play the Yankees. My father should have connected with Frank over sports—should have spent long afternoons with him playing catch or teaching him how to bunt—but it just wasn't that way.

Then, one night, my father came home from work and slammed the front door, a sure sign the dark cloud had descended. He made his way to Frank's room, pushed open the door, and started yelling. Frank cowered in his bed. My father reached for one of the trophies and twisted the little statue off its base. He threw the pieces to the floor and went for another one, destroying that one, too. He didn't stop until every last trophy had been wrenched in half or stomped or thrown against a wall. He left Frank to sleep in a pile of his jagged, broken trophies. The next time I looked in his bedroom—after I came back from school the next day—everything had been cleared away, and there were only empty shelves where once had been an army of little gold men.

It's hardly surprising that Frank didn't pursue sports in high school. In fact, he didn't even graduate.

Sometime around the tenth grade, Frank lost his way.

He started drinking too much and using drugs. When he was seventeen or eighteen, he went to Florida with some of his buddies, and he got into serious trouble there. I don't remember exactly what happened; I just know my parents had to bail him out of jail and replace a car he had totaled. He was not violent, just restless and sometimes reckless and even a little crazy here and there. I remember being at my parents' home in Long Island one night when Frank walked in, clearly stoned on something. He got into a screaming match with my father, and it got so heated that Frank did something completely out of character for him: he grabbed a kitchen knife and waved it at my father. I remember my mother begging Frank to stop, but it was my father—the man whose rages could not be interrupted—who defused the situation by stepping back and calming things down and letting Frank have the last word.

It was the first time I ever saw my father handle a crisis that way.

Not long after that fight, Frank agreed to enlist in the navy. That had been my mother's desperate wish for him. She saw how lost he was, and she thought regimen and routine would do him good. Frank, horrified he had been so stoned he would pull a knife on his father, agreed. In the service he got to see the world; I remember him excitedly describing the Seychelles Islands. I remember him surprising my mother with a really nice china service for twelve that he sent from the Philippines. She'd never had nice china, and Frank remembered that. She was so happy to get it, and he was so thrilled that she was.

After almost three years in the service, Frank left the navy three weeks before his time was up to come home and be with our ailing mother. She died just two weeks after he got home. Frank then went to work building airplane wings for a company called Republic Fairchild in Farmingdale, Long Island. He fell in love with a woman named Murlene and with her two young children, Darren and Toniette. He seemed to settle into a groove, a stable, happy life. He could be shy around adults, but he was great with children, and Darren and Toniette were crazy about him. He taught Darren to play sports and spent long afternoons with him tossing a football. Frank was always on the sideline rooting him on; he never missed any of Darren's games.

When Darren won trophies, Frank made sure he had a big shelf for them in his room where they could forever be admired.

But when Frank was in his thirties, Republic Fairchild moved its plant to Kansas, and he lost his job. A year later he split up with Murlene. The children were still there for him, and he was still like a father to them. For more than a year, Toniette even lived with Frank, but around that time, he began to drift away. He found odd jobs, but they never lasted. He put on weight—sometimes he was nearly a hundred pounds too heavy—then lost it, then put it back on. He finally moved to Florida to be near Annette, and her children were happy to have him around. He was funny and affectionate and gentle, the kind of guy you just want to hug, and if adults couldn't always see that innate sweetness in him, children certainly could.

When he was forty-one, he developed a serious cough. My sister thought it was just a bad cold; Frank, who never complained about anything, wasn't too worried. The truth is Frank was too heavy, and he smoked too much. He didn't take care of himself like he should have. It was almost as if he didn't feel he was worth the effort. He went into the hospital for a minor procedure; the doctors ran tests on him and told him his carbon monoxide level was sky high. They didn't let him leave and ran more tests. He called Annette, and when she got to the hospital, Frank asked her to go pick up a pizza for him.

"Are you crazy?" she said. "You can't eat that. You're in a hospital."

The doctors kept him overnight, and by the time Annette came back to see him the next morning he was on a respirator. He started running a high fever, and antibiotics weren't working. Doctors didn't know precisely what was wrong with him, and they never found out. They ran test after test and floated theory after theory, but they never nailed a diagnosis. A pulmonologist was stumped. A kidney doctor came up with nothing. All we knew was that Frank was in critical condition and getting worse. We all flew down to see him at different times, and when I first walked into his room, I was stunned. He was pale and overweight and wheezing. He was hooked up to a respirator and couldn't speak. Eventually, I flew back home, but Annette visited him twice a day for the next six weeks.

Then Annette called me one night and asked me to come down. "Please, I can't be here by myself," she said. I booked the first flight for the next morning. While I was waiting to board the plane, I got a call from Annette.

"Frank died," she said.

I remember feeling overwhelmed with sadness. We all were. Annette, especially, beat herself up pretty badly. Frank had moved to Florida to be closer to her and her family. She saw him as much as she possibly could, but she still felt she could have done more for him. She blamed herself for not seeing that his cough was serious. She felt that somehow she had let him down. That wasn't true at all. She had welcomed him with open arms when he moved to Florida, and when he died she was by his side, holding his hand. At Frank's funeral, Steven got up to speak, and he told Annette not to feel bad and that we all dearly loved Frank. Still, we all felt a certain amount of guilt, because we knew Frank had taken the worst abuse from my father. We felt that we had escaped much of it ourselves only at Frank's expense.

It was impossible not to think that the damage my father inflicted on him is what pushed Frank off course in his life.

Doctors never did come up with a cause of death. In the end, his body just gave out—his heart, his lungs, his spirit. This diagnostic void made it even easier to believe Frank had been doomed all along. Something inside him was broken, and he never got any kind of sure footing on this earth. Worst of all, he never believed he was as good and worthy a person as he was. My siblings and I sometimes talk about Frank and remember all the funny, quirky things about him: how his proudest possession was an aqua blue Volkswagen Beetle he bought brand new for $7,400 right when VW discontinued the model; how he loved the Mets and the Yankees and how Steven would mail him box scores when he was in the navy; how, as a kid, he'd pop in his eight-track tapes of the Beatles and sing along like a rock star.

Steven remembers the time when he was ten years old and in the fifth grade and was summoned to the principal's office over the loudspeaker. When he got to the office, there was Frank, then nineteen, with a stern look on his face.

"You're in so much trouble," he told Steven. "Mom and Dad are so mad at you."

He put Steven in his car and started driving home, but then he jumped on the Long Island Expressway and drove in the other direction.

"Where we going?" Steven asked.

"Just wait," Frank said.

Frank ended up taking him to Shea Stadium for the fifth game of the 1973 National League Championship series between the New York Mets and the Cincinnati Reds. The Mets won that game, 7–2, and, with that, won the series. Toward the end of the ninth inning, Frank took Steven down to the edge of the field so they could sneak on and celebrate.

"I don't know," Steven said. "We'll get in trouble."

"Come on," said Frank. "Just follow me."

After the last out, a thousand fans rushed the field and ran around cheering and screaming and pulling up clumps of grass, rounding the bases as if they'd hit home runs themselves. Two of the fans going crazy on the field were Steven and Frank, and it's nice to picture them there, romping on the emerald green grass, frozen in time, happy, carefree.

We brought Frank up from Florida, so he could be buried on Long Island. We were all surprised to discover that St. Patrick's Cemetery in Huntington, where my father and mother were buried, a third plot had already been bought and paid for. We hadn't known about it, and we never learned who bought it. Was it my father's idea? My mother's? And why just one extra plot? At the time Annette was married, and so was Nancy, and so was I. Steven was engaged. That left only Frank, out there on his own. Sometimes I think my mother may have anticipated that and insisted on the extra plot, so her son Frank could be there next to her.

He is buried there now, with our parents, beneath a flat stretch of grass beside a gently sloping hill.

After coming back from North Carolina, Maurice quit the bootleg jeans business and got a job as a security guard with the Doar Security company in the Bronx. He started out making $5.15 an hour, but within six months he was promoted to a supervisor. His bosses saw he was good with people and particularly good at defusing tense situations. For a while he was assigned to a Bureau of Welfare office, where people were constantly agitated and fights were not uncommon. Maurice knew how to calm things down.

"Listen, I know why you're here. I know your circumstances," he'd say. "I know you need this money. So you can either move on from this argument and stay in line and get your money now, or you can keep fighting and get kicked out and have to wait until next week."

He would say, "Think about what you're doing. Your next decision will determine what happens to you. It's in your hands."

Eventually, his salary got all the way up to to $18 an hour.

But Maurice had bigger goals in mind, so he went back to school.

He enrolled at the Brooklyn Adult Learning Center, and his plan was to study hard for two years, pass his General Educational Development exam, and get his high school diploma. Just two months into his studies, a teacher pulled him aside.

"Listen, Maurice, I think you're ready to take the GED test right now," he said.

Maurice said no thanks. This test meant everything to him—it would decide the very shape of his future, the direction of the rest of his life—and he felt he wasn't ready. But the teacher kept pushing.

Finally, Maurice showed up at Edward R. Murrow High School on Avenue L in Brooklyn and took out his sharp No. 2 pencils and got to work. The test covered everything: history, English, math, social studies. It was split over two days, and when it was over, Maurice was exhausted. He was also sure he failed.

So he went back to school and kept studying. A few months later he came home after school, and Michelle and the kids were there to greet him. He noticed they were all acting funny. Michelle sat him down for dinner and brought out his favorites—a big rack of barbecued ribs, collard greens, and corn bread—and after dinner she served him a big slice of cheesecake. Maurice asked, "What's going on? What's all this about?"

Junior came up to him and handed him a frame. Inside the frame was his GED diploma. It had come in the mail.

All at once, his wife and children yelled, "Congratulations!!"

Maurice bowed his head and cried.

But his high school equivalency degree was just a first step. Next was another dream he'd been harboring for a while. Maurice took the test to join the New York Police Department. He passed that, too.

He still needed two years of college to become a cop, so he enrolled at Medgar Evers College in Brooklyn. It was there, while studying education, that he came across a newspaper article about the fate of black youth in New York City. The article said there were more black men in prison than in college. Maurice got together with some other students and the president of the college and started the prison-to-college pipeline for the Male Development program, a campus organization designed to encourage young black men to get involved with their communities and realize their own strengths and potential.

The college president, Dr. Edison Jackson, was impressed with Maurice and asked him to give a speech at a budget litigation meeting in front of the New York City Council. On the day of the speech, Maurice got up early, put on a tie and jacket, and read his speech a dozen times. Outside the meeting room he took a deep breath to calm his nerves. When it was his turn, he sat in front of a microphone, cleared his throat, and started his speech. He flubbed a line, then flubbed another one. But then he calmed down.

"On behalf of Medgar Evers College, I implore the council to fund this program. We are ready to do whatever it takes to promote the development and progress of young black men."

Afterward Dr. Jackson put a hand on his shoulder and told him he had done a great job. He made Maurice a spokesman for the Male Development program. Before long, he was hired as a research director for a college program called the Fatherhood Initiative. He was awarded a Certificate of Achievement for outstanding work in his community and in school.

Right now, Maurice is halfway to earning his degree.

He is the first man in his family to earn even a single college credit.

19

THE GREATEST GIFT

Friday, October 5, 2001. The Westchester Country Club in Rye, New York. Close to ninety people in eveningwear fill a mahogany-paneled main room. Beautiful jewel flowers are scattered on every table. Everyone is there to celebrate a special occasion.

Laura Schroff—that's me—is turning fifty.

My husband, Michael, had been planning my birthday party for months. I had long since picked out the perfect dress, a beautiful black silk shantung creation from Bergdorf Goodman. My brother and sisters and their families were set to be there—the first time all of us would be together in more than five years. I had chosen a theme—Laura's Life in Music—and selected three songs from each decade of my life.

Three weeks before the party, the World Trade towers were attacked.

My first thought was to cancel the party, but in the days and weeks that followed, I came to realize there was no better time to celebrate our blessings—to say thanks for the family and friends who make our lives worth living. We agreed to have the party as planned, and everyone who was supposed to be there showed up.

It was a magical night. The pall of the 9/11 attacks made us all even more aware of how lucky we were to have one another. We had chosen music as my theme because it had so much meaning for my sisters and me growing up. I remembered playing records in the living room of my family's house in Huntington Station and dancing for hours with Annette to songs like Chubby Checker's "The Twist." Dancing was our escape then. And on this night, it was again.

We had drinks and dinner and then my birthday celebration after that. Michael, dashing in a tuxedo, toasted me, as did my friends Phoebe and Jules, my mother-in-law, Jean, and my sister Annette. When it was Steven's turn, he asked me to dance to "The Wonder of You." I remember feeling almost giddy with happiness. Here I was, surrounded by the people I loved most in the world. I felt a deep sense of appreciation for everything I had. It's not often you get the chance to step back from your life, survey the landscape you have traveled, and say thanks to the people you have traveled it with, reflecting on how truly fortunate you are. Sure, people say nice things about you at your funeral, but you're not there to hear them. I had a chance not only to hear them, but to say thank you to them, and it was a night I will never forget.

Then came the final toast. The speaker was in a sharp black

tuxedo with spectacular black-and-white shoes, and his wife was in a stunning navy blue gown, her hair swept up. Nearly everyone in the room had met him or at least knew his story, and so everyone was excited to see him and hear him speak. He kissed his wife, walked up and took the microphone, and began his toast.

"Laurie, where can I start," Maurice began. "We met . . . the way we met was so special to me. I was a young boy on the street with barely nothing, and I was very hungry that day and I asked this lady, 'Miss, can you spare some change?' And she walked away. And then she stopped. She was in the middle of the street—she almost got hit—and she looked and came back and took me to McDonald's. We ate and then walked around Central Park; she took me to Häagen-Dazs and then we played some games.

"You know, at that moment she saved my life. 'Cause I was going down the wrong road, the wrong hill, and, you know, my mother—bless her soul, my mother died—and she was on drugs at the time, and the Lord sent me an angel. And my angel was Laurie.

"Without you," Maurice said, raising his glass, "I could not be the man I am today."

I was so incredibly moved when I heard Maurice say I saved his life. Heck, I nearly lost it throughout his whole darn toast. Whenever I hear someone tell me how lucky Maurice is to have met me, I have to stop them and correct them. The truth is that the lucky one is me.

Maurice taught me so many things; I can't possibly list them all. He taught me how to live. He taught me one of the most important lessons a person can hope to learn—he taught me to be grateful for what I have. He taught me about resilience, courage, perseverance, and about the special strength that comes from overcoming adversity. He taught me the true value of money, the real meaning of lunch in a brown paper bag, the importance of a silly ritual like baking cookies. He taught me, more than I ever taught him, what it means to be a friend.

Everything I ever gave to Maurice, he gave back to me tenfold. Every meal, every shirt, every bike or toothbrush, was matched by Maurice with a more genuine appreciation than I have ever known. Every hand I ever lent him was returned with a hug; every kindness was paid back with an impossibly optimistic smile. If love is the greatest gift of all—and I believe it is—then the greatest privilege of all is to be able to love someone. Maurice appeared out of nowhere and allowed me to love him, and for that, I simply can never thank him enough. His generosity of spirit continues to astound me, and to this day my relationship with him is the relationship I am most proud of in my life.

About a year after my fiftieth birthday party, Michael and I divorced. Perhaps my resentments about Maurice lingered. And I'm not sure we ever got past our disagreements about having a child. I remember I finally settled on getting a dog instead, and Michael disagreed with me about that, too. Finally I put my foot down and announced I was getting a little red French poodle, and I was going to name her Lucy, and if he didn't like it that was too bad. And that's just what I did. Lucy—my lovely little Lucy—helped me get over the pain I felt at not being able to have a child. Two years later I gave Lucy a sister, an adorable poodle named Coco. When I was growing up, the pets in my life came and went, but Lucy and Coco were never anything less than my family.

Michael loved my "girls" as much as I did, but eventually we just got off track. Divorce is never just one person's fault. Michael and I had wonderful times together, and in many ways he was a wonderful husband and even the love of my life. I'm sure we will always remain friends, but now I am on my own. I feel good and strong and happy about life and more hopeful than ever about what lies ahead. I finally retired from the advertising business after a long and successful career, and I feel so blessed to have been surrounded by so many amazing people who are still my friends today. Every once in a while I get the itch to jump back into it, but I doubt I will. I think it's just time to try new things.

I eventually sold my apartment in Manhattan and moved down to Florida for a while, but I got restless and came right back. I'd like to buy another place in the city someday soon, but more than anything, I want to take a cruise with my whole family: with Annette and Bruce; with my niece Colette, who's all grown up now, and her husband, Mike, and their daughter, Calli; with my nephew, Derek, and his wife, Brooke, and their son, Dashiell; with my niece Brooke and her boyfriend, Steve; with Nancy and John and their daughter, Jena, and son, Christian; with my little brother, Steven, who I love so much; and, of course, with Maurice, his lovely wife, Michelle, and their remarkable children.

I don't care where we sail to or what we do. I only care that we are all together on that boat.

I'd like to keep seeing my friend Maurice, if not every Monday, then as often as possible. Looking back on our relationship, I am struck by how unusual it was. We hailed from such vastly different worlds, and on the surface, at least, we had very little in common. There was so much about Maurice's life I didn't know. Only very recently, for instance, did I learn that when I met him Maurice was actually twelve years old, and not eleven as we had always thought. He did not consistently celebrate his birthday as a child, and he may not have even known his real age when I met him. It was only when we started working on this book together that he figured out how old he was back then. I did not make the correction earlier in these pages, because that would not be true to the way the story unfolded for Maurice and I. The point is, there are many things that separate the two of us—age, culture, circumstance—and from the outside we might not seem like your typical close friends.

But I can honestly say no friendship is more important to me— none closer to my heart—than my friendship with Maurice.

After leaving Medgar Evers College, Maurice decided he didn't want to be a cop after all. He went into the construction business, and he's now trying to get his own small construction firm—Moe's Finest Contracting, LLC—off the ground. He goes into old buildings, guts them, and puts in new pipes and wires and walls. He is incredibly talented, and I have no doubt his business will be a great success. He is already able to hire some employees.

In 2010, when Uncle Old got out of prison, Maurice gave him a job.

But the thing that makes me most proud of Maurice is his family. He has been with Michelle for eighteen years now. He says he is more in love with her now than he has ever been. After his mother died, Maurice and his sisters each received a few hundred dollars in benefits. Maurice used some of that money to buy an engagement

engagement ring for Michelle. They got married in front of a justice of the peace—just the two of them and two witnesses. If his business ever really takes off, he plans to give Michelle a real wedding.

And then there are his children. When I finally met them, I instantly fell in love with all of them. I mean, they are *incredible* kids—so bright, so vibrant, so funny, and overflowing with dreams. Maurice has become a father to Michelle's son, Ikeem, who is twenty and tall and handsome. He thinks he might want to join the army one day. And there is Maurice's firstborn, Junior, now seventeen and taller than his dad. His goal is to become a cook. There is Jalique, sixteen, a carbon copy of Maurice at that age; he wants to be a detective. Jahleel, eleven, likes the idea of being a police officer but also loves playing chess. Maurice has two daughters, too, and the first one he named Princess. She is fourteen and nicknamed "MaMa" and "YaYa." She applied to the Fashion Institute of Technology and hopes to have a career in fashion marketing and design. She is beautiful and a natural charmer. Her sister is Precious, who is eight and enamored with jumping rope and Miley Cyrus. She wants to be a veterinarian and maybe an actress on the side. "I want to go on adventures," she says.

And there is Maurice's youngest, Jahmed, who is four. He's a ball of energy who loves professional wrestling, just like his father does; he'll show you his replica championship belt and hoist it high above his head in a fierce wrestling pose. It looks like he's got a ton of musical talent, too, particularly for drumming. I remember Maurice handing him two pencils and watching him tap out an amazing arrangement on the table. "I also know how to make pancakes," he says.

I cannot get over how sweet and smart and sparkling Maurice's children are—and what a strong, loving, patient father he is. I see him teasingly try to swipe a candy bar that Princess is holding or wait two hours for Jahleel at a chess tournament or scoop up little Jahmed and sit with him in his lap for a while, and I marvel at how giving and affectionate he is. Maurice offers some of the credit for his parenting instincts to his mother and his grandmother. When he is in the kitchen on Thanksgiving, he says he talks to Darcella and Grandma Rose, and he tells them about his kids. If he listens closely enough he can almost hear them talking back to him, telling him to watch out for this or take care of that. And in that way they teach him to be a good father.

Maurice has also served as a mentor to children in community youth groups, and he is starting a volunteer group that helps disadvantaged kids—acts of kindness that take him full circle from his days on the streets.

"I consider my childhood a gift," Maurice once told me. "It happened to me so I could learn the right way to raise my children. I saw what my father did, and I might have grown up thinking that was the only way to handle children, like my father handled me. But then I met you, and that's when I realized there was another way."

I remember one of the first times I went to Maurice's apartment to see him and his family. He and Michelle had moved after twelve years in the same apartment in Brooklyn and were now living on Madison Street, in downtown Manhattan. Some people might consider the building run-down, but Maurice sees it differently.

"Compared to the way I grew up," he says, "I live like a king now." That is why he named his daughter Princess—"because," he says, "I think of her as royalty."

His apartment is a fairly nice size and is filled with laundry and toys and stray sneakers. Through the living room window you can see not only the Manhattan Bridge but, just beyond it, the Brooklyn Bridge. It is a breathtaking view, almost epic, suggesting promise and adventure. On one wall there are framed pictures of the children, on another a small flat-screen TV. There is also an Xbox, so Maurice can school his children in the art of video games just as he schooled me all those years ago.

And then I saw it.

It was in the living room, which doubles as a dining room, and when I saw it, Maurice smiled with pride.

A really big dining room table.

It was so big it went nearly from wall to wall, and eight chairs fit easily around it. If he needed to, Maurice could even add an extension or two and make it bigger. That's where Maurice and his wife and his children have their meals, talk about their days, kid one another about this and that, and make plans to go to birthday parties and ball games and chess matches, where Jahmed, if he is in the mood, will do a little drumming with his No. 2 pencils.

"You see," Maurice said to me, beaming, "I told you I'd get a big table someday."

And then I sat down at that table and had dinner with my family.

EPILOGUE: LOVE, MAURICE

Dear Laurie:

I'm writing this letter to let you know the impact you've had on my life. When I look back on everything that's happened, I realize that if I hadn't met you, I would not be the man I am today. I am eternally grateful for the love and care that you've shown me through the years. You've taught me how to dream, how to trust people, how to be a productive member of society, and, most of all, how to be a good man and a great father.

It all began on that day long ago when I asked you for money, and you walked right by me. At that moment, Laurie, I'm sure I thought you were just another one of those rich, uppity white people I'd always been told about.

But then you came back, and now I realize how black-and-white my world was before I met you. The beliefs that I'd been raised on were based on only one point of view. My mother and my grandmother were brought up in a time of segregation. That, coupled with a lack of education, is a recipe for distrust. When I first started seeing you, my grandmother would say, "You'd better stay away from that white bitch." But in time, once she saw how I was benefitting from our relationship, she started saying things like, "That lady really cares about you," and, "How's that lady doing? Are you gonna see her again soon?" My grandmother went from flat-out not trusting or respecting you to believing you were a guardian angel God sent to watch over me.

I remember you asking me what I wanted to be when I grew up. At that point, I'd never looked that far down the road; I just lived from day to day. I was more worried about what I was going to eat the next day than about what I wanted to be when I grew up. I didn't know if I even would grow up, given the way I was living, but after meeting you, I began to broaden my view on my life. I began to think I could actually get a job of some kind. For the first time ever, I could picture myself as an adult, and maybe even see myself working as a police officer.

Even then, though, there was a problem, and that was how much I doubted myself. I doubted myself because I'd always been told I was illiterate. I was a bad student in school, so I was given an Individualized Education Program evaluation. My mother attended my IEP evaluation, and for some reason she came out believing I couldn't read or write. My entire family began to tell me I couldn't read or write. I knew that I could read and I also knew that I could write, although I wrote very slowly, but because I was constantly teased and reminded that I was illiterate, I began to think that it didn't matter if I could or couldn't—that

I was destined to live the kind of life the rest of the men in my family had.

And then, Laurie, you came to my rescue again. Just when I thought I was doomed, just when that first dream you encouraged me to dream had been all but shattered, you told me about how you struggled in school when you were my age. I can't tell you how much your sharing that meant to me. I started to think that if someone like you—a person who was so articulate, who had such abundance in her life—could have experienced hardships of her own and overcome them, then so could I. After that, I completely ignored anyone who would sing the song of my incompetence. I decided that your opinion of me was fact, and anyone who didn't agree with it was just plain jealous or unhappy with themselves. That mind-set changed everything for me. To this day, it still helps me deal effectively with issues in my life. To this day, it gives me the courage to dare to dream.

Laurie, there are so many things you taught me, so many experiences I could never have had if it weren't for you. I remember all the times you took me to see your sister's family on Long Island, but a couple of visits stand out. I remember the day your niece Brooke was crying hysterically when she found out Santa Claus wasn't real. I remember thinking, "Uh-oh, she'd better be quiet before she gets a beating." I remember seeing her father, Bruce, come in and thinking, "Aw, man, time for her whipping." But to my great surprise, and delight, all he did was console and comfort his daughter. He picked her up and wiped her tears, and he whispered something in her ear and then gave her a hug and that was that. I remember thinking Bruce was the best father in the world, and I learned something about being a father that day.

The next visit that stands out is the first time we all sat down at your sister's big dining room table. I honestly didn't know that tables came that big, but that's not what fascinated me. It wasn't the food or the nice silverware, either. What really intrigued me was all the love that was passed across that table. There was one story after another and so much laughter. It's a feeling I couldn't explain back then, but now I know that feeling is called family. It's a feeling I get every night when I am with my wife and children.

Because of you, Laurie, I got to see the many different ways people show they love and care for each other. I'm thinking of all those lunches you prepared for me and put in those brown paper bags. I realize some people might not understand why the paper bags were important. But to me, they showed that someone had taken the time to make me lunch. Someone had actually thought of me; someone cared about me. Laurie, you took the time to make my lunches and you showed me that you cared about me, and all those kids at school could see that someone cared about me, too. I just can't thank you enough for all those brown paper bags.

The times we spent together were the best times of my life. I had tons of fun playing games and hanging out, but I also learned more with you than I ever did anywhere else. I didn't realize it then, but as I've gotten older I've started to notice that all those little life lessons I picked up are a guiding force in my life today. Lessons like, "You don't have to fight all the time to prove how tough you are, Maurice." Do you remember telling me that? Maybe you don't. But I'll never forget it. You showed me it was more important to be mentally tough than physically tough, and that is a lesson I try to impart to my own children today.

Finally, and this is important, I want you to know why I disappeared and didn't contact you for all that time. Back then, I wanted to tell you what was really going on in my life, but I felt I couldn't. I knew you were unhappy that I had a child so young, and I couldn't tell you I had a second child, too. The thing I hated more than anything was disappointing you, not after all you'd done for me. I also felt you had taught me all I needed to know to make something of myself. So I stopped calling you, and I went out into the world on my own. And, Laurie, I was right: the things you taught me wound up saving my life.

When I finally called you again, I reentered your life as a man, not a boy. I lived, and I loved, and I had children, and I've taught my children all the things that you taught me. And, most importantly, I love them just as much as you love me.

I know An Invisible Thread *is about an unusual friendship between two different people, but I think it is about much more than that. It is about a mother longing for a child and a child longing for a mother. That longing had nothing to do with umbilical cords or DNA. It had to do with two people who needed each other and who were destined to meet on the corner of 56th Street and Broadway. Every Monday, that mother got to know her son, and that son learned about his mother.*

And on those Mondays their hearts were sewn together with an invisible thread.

I love you, Mom,

Maurice Mozell

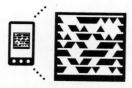

Get the free mobile app at
http://gettag.mobi

To watch a video of Maurice's toast at Laura's fiftieth birthday party, simply download the free Microsoft Tag app at http://gettag.mobi.

Then scan the TAG with your phone's camera to watch the video.

Click it. Watch it.

Howard authors on your Smartphone.

To share your own Invisible Thread story, please visit www.aninvisiblethread.com.

ACKNOWLEDGMENTS

How do I begin to thank Maurice for coming into my life and changing it forever? Over the years, many people have told me how lucky Maurice was to have met me, but my response was always, "No, I was lucky to have met *him*." Maurice, you have brought so much joy into my life and showed me in many ways the true meaning of *friendship*, and for that all I can say is, "Thank you, with all my heart." Thank you also to Maurice's wife and my dear friend Michelle, for being there for Maurice when I was not. I am so proud of the two of you and your exceptional, loving family.

My very deepest thanks to my dear mother, for her amazing strength and unconditional love, and to my father, who was great when he was good. You for showed me the true meaning of hard work. Because of what you instilled in me, I was able to have a remarkable career in advertising. And, to my brother Frank, who is at peace and will always be dearly loved. I think of you every day.

There is an old saying, "You can pick your friends, but you can't pick your family." That may be true, but I couldn't have chosen sisters and brothers more wonderful than the ones I have. Annette Lubsen, Nancy Johansen, and Steven Carino—thank you for allowing me to open up our lives and share our story with the world. Most important, thank you for the incredible support and love you have shown me not only through this entire process but throughout my entire life.

To my brother-in-law Bruce Lubsen, thank you for showing Maurice how important it is to be an understanding, loving, and comforting father. You had a tremendous impact on Maurice, and you play an integral role in his life today. To Colette Lubsen-Reid, Brooke Lubsen, and Jena Johansen, my sweet and loving nieces, you have been there for me every step of the way. Your constant interest and support is incredible, and I love you all very much. To my brother-in-law John Johansen and my nephews Christian Johansen and Derek Lubsen—we are so proud of all of you. To my mother's sister and brother, Aunt Diana Robedee and Uncle Pat Procino, thank you for always keeping us close in your hearts.

The name of this book is relevant to another special relationship in my life. My coauthor Alex and I worked together for seventeen years at Time Inc., and our paths never crossed. He was on the edit side and I was in advertising, but through the help of my friend Martha Nelson, we were brought together. Thank you, Alex, for recognizing the power of my story and for committing to help me tell it. Just like Maurice, you were someone I was destined to meet, and

I'd like to think that, once again, this was my mother orchestrating from high above.

A very special thank-you to my dear friend and mentor Valerie Salembier, who wrote the beautiful, heartfelt foreword for this book. You were the first person I told about my new friend, and I thank you for believing I knew what I was doing. Your love, support, and friendship over thirty-plus years have been simply incredible.

So many people have untold stories, and without our powerful literary agent our story would have stayed untold, too. To Jan Miller, thank you for believing our book could make a difference. There aren't enough words to express my gratitude to you. You and your team at Dupree/Miller have been so incredibly supportive, and it is an honor to work with you all.

A very special thanks to Nena Madonia, for her relentless support and for helping to make sure *An Invisible Thread* found the right home. Nena, you have been such a remarkable partner through this entire process. I am so proud to call you not only my agent but, more important, my very dear friend.

The right home for a book makes all the difference, and how lucky for us that Jonathan Merkh and Becky Nesbitt at Howard Books not only embraced our story but did so with such passion. You loved it from the beginning. I will always be indebted to the both of you, and I cannot thank all of you enough. Jessica Wong, our talented editor, what can I say about your unyielding support and obvious love for our story? Thank you for making our journey an extraordinary and seamless one. You have been our champion. A special thanks to the brilliant and talented team at Howard Books, especially Betty Woodmancy and Jennifer Smith.

ACKNOWLEDGMENTS

A very special thank-you to all of my friends at Time Inc. To Martha Nelson, whom I met at *Ms.* magazine—how lucky and happy I am that our paths continued to cross throughout my career. You have always been there for me, and I thank you for helping me connect with Alex. To Paul Caine, who remembers my early days with Maurice and who has always been a true champion of our relationship. I can't say how much I appreciate your constant encouragement. To David Geithner, who has shown enormous enthusiasm for my story, and to his colleagues Rebecca Sanhueza and Nancy Valentino. And a special mention to the amazing PR team of Sandi Shurgin-Werfel and Heidi Krupp.

To all of my friends at *USA Today* who were so supportive of my relationship with Maurice, thank you. A special thanks to Lou and Donna Cona, who had such empathy for Maurice—and brought him bags of clothing when he needed them most.

Teachers are paid to teach, but in the case of Miss Kim House, she did more than teach—she cared. Thank you for the enormous compassion you showed Maurice and for how you went above and beyond the call of duty. I commend you, and so should the highest powers in the New York City school system because, in you, they have someone who has made a real difference in the lives of children.

I believe people come into our lives for a reason, and that is the case with my very dear friend and advisor Laura Lynne Jackson. Thank you for sharing your very special gift with me. Your words of encouragement, insight, and support helped me believe our book would happen. When there was no word, you kept encouraging me to enjoy the downtime—you called it the calm before the storm.

And you were so right! You have brought an enormous amount of peace and comfort into my life.

Over many, many years I've been so blessed with the great gift of friendship. Friends do not come in beautiful blue boxes with white satin bows; they just show up and change your life. To all of the dear friends who have been there through so many of my ups and downs, I can only hope I repaid a fraction of the love and support you gave me. A heartfelt thank-you to Christina Albee and Gregg Goldsholl and sweet Clare, Lori Cohn, June Deane, Susan Egan, Mary Gallagher-Vassilakos, Susan Goldfarb, Barbara Groner-Robinton, Cherie and Joseph Guccione, Scott Jacobs, Lori Ressa-Kyle, Nora and Ed McAniff, Darcy Parriott-Phillips, Mary Phillips, Brette Popper and Paul Spraos, Lauren Price, Andrea Rogan, Phoebe Rothkopf, Kim Schechter, Janet Shechter, Lori Levine-Silver, Donna Smith, Sue and John Spahlinger, Pam Stanger, Stacie Sullivan, Lynn Ruane-Tuttle, Michael Wellner, and Kevin White. Thank you also to my friend and hairdresser, Liell Hilligoss at Pierre Michel, and to my photographer, Joseph Moran.

Finally, I'd like to thank all of you, the readers of this book. I hope you, too, will look at your own lives and think about how an invisible thread has connected you to the special people in your lives. I believe it does not happen by accident.

Laura Schroff

I feel incredibly lucky to have had Laura Schroff and Maurice Mazyck come into my life. Laura, thank you so much for trusting me to help tell your remarkable story. I'm in awe of your generous heart and beautiful spirit, and the way you live your life is an inspiration.

ACKNOWLEDGMENTS

Maurice, my fellow Knicks fan, I'm blown away by your strength and courage and conviction, and by your beautiful wife and children. You are a hero to me.

Thank you to Larry Hackett and everyone else at *People Magazine* for letting me come in so late. Thank you to Martha Nelson, for endless support. Thank you to my great friend Susan Schindehette, simply the best, most graceful writer I know, and to everyone at MiWorld.com—you guys are the future. Thank you to the folks at Howard Books, especially Jonathan Merkh, Becky Nesbitt, and Jessica Wong. Thank you, Jan Miller and Nena Madonia, for being the best agents I've ever had, and easily the nicest, too. Thank you, Mark Apovian, for the mulligans.

Thank you to Art and Nola Chester, for being such giving and lovely friends. A heartfelt thanks to my sister Tam, for her amazing generosity, and my sister Fran, for always being there to bail me out, and my brother Nick, who is my oldest and best friend. Thank you, Zach and Emily, for growing into such cool and amazing people—I love you both a ton—and to Gracie and Willie, who have a special place in my heart and always will. Thank you to my little ones—Manley, Guy, LiLi, Nino, and SheShe, I love you like crazy. Thank you to my wonderful friends Amy and Neil and Angie and Karen and Greg and of course Lindsay. And thank you, as always, to Lorraine Stundis, who gave me key suggestions that made all the difference in this project. Rainey, you're my rock.

Alex Tresniowski

A CONVERSATION WITH LAURA SCHROFF

What made you want to write down your experience with Maurice and share it with others?

In 1997, *Good Housekeeping* wrote a short article about my relationship with Maurice, and I received an overwhelming response from friends and colleagues in the ad community. I was continually told I should write a book and document our story. People loved the story and wanted to know more. But it was not until 2007, after I took an early retirement package from Time Inc. and moved to Florida, that I had enough time to begin contemplating the book. In the first few years that I was friends with Maurice, it never dawned on me that our story would be of any interest to other people, but as I started working on the book with my coauthor Alex Tresniowski, I began to realize there was a powerful message in the experiences Maurice and I shared. And so I became determined to share our story with the world.

What were some of the challenges of writing *An Invisible Thread*? What did you enjoy most about this experience?

I knew from the very beginning I needed someone like Alex to help me write my book. I mean, I knew what I wanted to say, and I knew what message I wanted the book to have, but I needed someone to help me shape and structure the story. It's amazing to me how much effort and research goes into creating a book. The challenge for me was remaining faithful to the experiences Maurice and I shared while also making the story as dramatic and compelling for readers as possible. I wanted the book to convey how amazing and emotional and miraculous it was that Maurice and I found each other. It was also a challenge to relive all of the difficult moments of my childhood. That was harder and sadder than I thought it would be. But it was also kind of a blessing to be able to revisit my childhood and put it in some kind of context.

What I enjoyed most about the process of writing *An Invisible Thread* was just that—the process. Sometimes I still find it hard to believe our story will be read by so many people and hopefully have an impact on people's lives. Reliving my incredible friendship with Maurice, his wife, Michelle, and their children, and working with Alex, has been nothing less than remarkable. There are no words to describe the support I received from my family and friends and how truly fortunate I am. It has been the most astonishing experience of my life, and it confirms to me, and I hope to all of you too, how important it is to dream big dreams, as dreams really do come true. You must know that I was really the least likely person to ever publish a book, and yet here I am.

Did you ever second-guess the friendship you had with Maurice? Did comments and concerns from friends ever make you reevaluate your instincts?

You know, maybe I should have, but the truth is I never did. I knew the very first time I met Maurice that he was a very special child; he had the most trusting face and eyes. In the early stages of our friendship, my friends and family urged me to be careful and told me all the reasons I shouldn't be doing what I was doing. But I just always believed Maurice was a really good kid in a truly horrific situation, and that he came into my life for a special reason. And Maurice never gave me a single reason to doubt or mistrust him, so I never really questioned what I was doing.

Going into your marriage with Michael, why didn't you make it clear to him that you wanted to have children? And did having Maurice in your life make it easier to deal with the disappointment of not having a child?

Michael and I were just so compatible, and we were having so much fun getting to know each other, that I guess I just didn't want to complicate things by bringing up the matter of children. Obviously, in retrospect, this was a big mistake, and I would urge every couple to have these serious conversations prior to getting married. But I was so deliriously happy to have met Michael, and to have this second chance at happiness, that it never dawned on me that we would not have a family of our own. Ultimately, when I turned forty-four,

I realized having a child at my age could be a selfish act on my part. By then, Michael and I would both be older parents, and I believed it would be unfair to the child. After all, I lost my mother when I was only twenty-five, and I knew firsthand how difficult it was not to have a mother in those later years. And so, finally, I gave up the dream of having a child. Was it painful? Very much so. If I think about it for too long, it still makes me sad. And, no, having Maurice in my life did not immediately help me deal with the grief I felt about not having a child. You see, I was feeling a lot of guilt about marrying Michael and moving up to Westchester, which fundamentally changed the nature of my relationship with Maurice. And so, in a way, I had to deal with the pain of losing Maurice and not having a child all at the same time. But prior to my meeting Michael, and now, at this point in my life, Maurice was and is the child I always wanted and dreamed of having.

How do you think your life would be different if you had never turned around that day you met Maurice?

Quite simply, my life would be a lot emptier had I not turned around that day. I mean, there's just so much pleasure and happiness that Maurice has brought into my life, and just so many ways he changed how I thought about my life and particularly my childhood. The times we spent together just talking, baking cookies, and doing our Monday night rituals were incredibly rewarding. He didn't realize it then, and neither did I, but he was a child teaching an adult the true meaning of love and trust and friendship. I used to say to my family and friends all the time that we all need to meet a child like Maurice to help open up our eyes and to see how truly fortunate we are and how the other half lives. It sounds kind of selfish, but Maurice helped me deal with a lot of difficult issues in my life, a lot of difficult memories. And of all my achievements in life, there is nothing that makes me feel more proud than to call Maurice my friend and the son I never had. I can only hope he has gotten as much out of our relationship as I have.

Why was it so important for you to maintain a certain distance between you and Maurice, such that you only wanted to remain his friend and not create a mother-son dynamic? How did this ultimately shape your relationship?

Early on I believed it was very important for me not to try to replace Maurice's mother. The truth is, he had a mother, and he loved her very much, and I am sure she loved him very much. And I did not want to change that, or get in the way of Maurice's relationship with his mother. Perhaps she wasn't always there for him, and she made bad choices, but I wasn't living in her shoes and I didn't understand the challenges she was facing, and so I never wanted to make life any harder for her. All I wanted was to help Maurice in any way I could, as a friend. And I know to this day Maurice loves his mother and is proud of her for doing what she could to raise her children. And I am so glad that he is.

But as our relationship developed, I can't deny that we developed a mother-son bond. In fact, just the way I am around him, even today, telling him to do this or that, reminding him to be on time—I'm very mothering with him, and he's thirty-six now! Even back then, there were times I thought about what it would be like to adopt Maurice, and have him come live with me, and of course I dreamed that Michael and I would take him into our home. But I think our relationship played out exactly as it was supposed to play out. I think because I didn't try to replace his mother, we were able to become great friends as well as a kind of mother and son.

You often remark on how wonderful it was to witness Maurice experience the simple pleasure of childhood experiences. Were you afforded these same joys as a child? Were there any experiences you wanted to give to Maurice that you yourself never had?

Our experiences growing up were very different. As a child in a middle-class family I never worried about having a toothbrush, or where my next meal would come from, or having a winter coat or a bed to sleep in. For Maurice, the joys I gave him were the ones I took for granted. I was blessed with a very strong and loving mother and a hard-working father who kept a roof over our heads. I know now and I knew back then that my childhood was very different from my friends' childhoods. But in our own dysfunctional way my family was a loving family, with an enormous amount of support. But there was one thing neither Maurice nor I had as young children, and that was a sense of security, a place to escape the chaos. And that's what I wanted to give Maurice when I met him—a feeling that he had some place to go where he was safe and protected and loved and cared for.

How do you think your family upbringing affected the way you interacted with Maurice?

I believed it was essential to give Maurice as much structure as possible through our weekly rituals, as this was something I yearned for as a child. I wanted things to be the same, to not change, to not have to move all the time and see our lives turned upside down. That's probably one of the most important messages of the book—the value of simple little rituals in a child's life. Consistency was something I thought about often and tried to provide Maurice. My father was a great father some of the time and a bad father some of the time. And I wanted to consistently be there for Maurice, to be dependable.

However, the most important thing I wanted to give Maurice was confidence. I truly believe it is one of the most important gifts parents or a caregiver can give a child. As hard as my upbringing was, and even though I was a terrible student, somewhere along the way I became an extremely confident person. I'm not sure how, but I did. And my poor brother Frank—he never developed that confidence because of the relationship he had with our father. And in many ways that lack of confidence doomed him. I believe confidence is what helps you dream and achieve those dreams, so I wanted Maurice to know how extraordinary he was, and for him to want something different for himself and ultimately for his family some day. Maurice was such an insightful child, such a smart boy, and one of the biggest obstacles in his life was that no one had ever told him that. You have to tell your children over and over how special they are, and no one did that for Maurice. I really believe if children have one person they can truly count on and who they know truly loves them, it makes all the difference in their life. I hoped I could be that one person for Maurice.

You write that your mother was the guiding light that directed you toward Maurice. How would she have felt about Maurice?

My mother would have absolutely loved Maurice. She would have been so proud of his character, his strength, and his ability to understand at a very young age the power of right and wrong. She would have admired how he had the innate awareness to want to take his life down a different path and how he had the perseverance to overcome the difficult challenges he faced. I also think how my mother would have respected Maurice for never trying to sabotage a good thing because he felt he was not deserving of our friendship. I mean, he could have easily done something to mess up our friendship because he just didn't believe it was real or that it could last. I always marveled at how Maurice knew at such a young age that our meeting each other was such an incredible gift for the both of us. And of course I believe it was my mother who brought us together, so I'm sure she would love him and embrace him and appreciate him just like I do.

In the beginning of your story, you described the "invisible thread" that bound you and Maurice together. Would you consider that fate? Do you believe in things like providence, fate, and destiny?

I consider myself an extremely spiritual person, and I have no doubt fate and destiny played a role in our lives. A few years ago, a very wise and dear friend told me, "It's not your lot in life to have your own children, but in fact to touch many." I hope I have done that in very simple loving ways with Maurice, his children, my nieces, nephews, and hopefully with my little great-niece and great-nephew too. If our story can make a difference for some children and adults, it will confirm that our special bond was meant to happen for a reason. Maurice and I hope our story can change how society thinks about people who are less fortunate and can help them to understand why it's sometimes nearly impossible to change a devastating cycle. If *An Invisible Thread* achieves this goal in some small way, then our friendship will have had more of a purpose than just what it gave to the two of us. So, yes, I believe in destiny, and I believe that's why Maurice and I found each other—to not only help each other, but hopefully to touch other people as well.

Do you have plans to write another book?

Working on *An Invisible Thread* has been more than I could have ever dreamed of. I am enjoying every moment of the experience, while continually counting my blessings. So I feel wonderfully happy to have this moment and to have had this journey. But I have been thinking about how great it would be to give other people a chance to share their "Invisible Thread" stories, and I think that would make a wonderful book—all of these stories of people who were destined to meet, and the amazing confluence of events that had to happen for them to meet, and how meeting each other changed their lives in profound ways. I think a lot of people out there have just such a person in their lives, and maybe they haven't really thought about their relationship as an "Invisible Thread" relationship, but maybe that's just what it is—this bond that bends but never breaks, connecting them for a reason. So I would love to be able to work on a book about other people's "Invisible Thread" stories.